The
5-Minute
BIBLE
STUDY
for
Uncertain
Times

ISBN 978-1-64352-943-1

Published by Barbour Publishing, Inc., 1810 Barbour Drive, Uhrichsville, Ohio 44683, www.barbourbooks.com

Our mission is to inspire the world with the life-changing message of the Bible.

Member of the
Evangelical Christian
Publishers Association

Printed in the United States of America.

The
5-Minute
BIBLE
STUDY
for
Uncertain
Times

Glenn Hascall

BARBOUR
PUBLISHING

INTRODUCTION

Do you find it hard to make time for Bible study? You intend to do it, but the hours turn into days and before you know it, another week has passed and you have not picked up God's Word. This book provides an avenue for you to open the Bible regularly and dig into a passage—even if you only have five minutes!

Minutes 1–2: *Read.* Carefully read the scripture passage for each day's Bible study.

Minute 3: *Understand.* Ponder a couple of prompts designed to help you apply the verses from the Bible to your own life. Consider these throughout your day as well.

Minute 4: *Apply.* Read a brief devotional based on the day's scripture. Think about what you are learning and how to apply the scriptural truths to your own life.

Minute 5: *Pray.* A prayer starter will help you to begin a time of conversation with God. Remember to allow time for Him to speak into your life as well.

May *The 5-Minute Bible Study for Uncertain Times* help you to establish the discipline of studying God's Word. Pour yourself a cup of coffee and make those first five minutes of your day count! You will find that even five minutes focused on scripture and prayer have the power to make a huge difference. Soon you will be craving even more time in God's Word!

FAULT LINES

Read Genesis 3:1–19

Key Verse:

*Then the man and his wife heard the sound of
the Lord God as he was walking in the garden
in the cool of the day, and they hid from the
Lord God among the trees of the garden.*

Genesis 3:8 niv

Understand:

- *How have you excused the sin you've chosen
  to commit?*

- *Why is it easier to blame others for the
  choices you make than to accept responsibility
  for them?*

Apply:

It was the best of times, then the worst of times. This
was the first of all uncertain times. Perfection had
been tossed aside for a forbidden taste. One man,
one woman, one rule. They couldn't eat fruit from a
particular tree. They did. Things changed. They were
embarrassed for the first time. They invented the
blame game, and no one was left out. They hid from

God. They lost their home.

Disregarding God's law invites days of uncertainty. The good news is God never leaves, but there will always be an ugly chain reaction when sin is the guest of honor.

This event established a new normal for all of mankind—*uncertain times*. God brings certainty to decision-making. Don't leave Him out of your next uncertain moment.

Pray:

I try to excuse my sin, but all it does is keep me from You. There are no acceptable reasons to sin. You said that if I break one of Your laws, it's no different than breaking all of them. The penalty is the same, and Your Son paid that price when He died on the cross. Keep me from keeping a personal sin collection. Help me admit You were right so I can rediscover forgiveness.

THE GREATEST CERTAINTY
Read Romans 5:12-21

Key Verse:

*Adam's sin led to condemnation, but God's free
gift leads to our being made right with God,
even though we are guilty of many sins.*
ROMANS 5:16 NLT

Understand:

- *Why might you feel uncomfortable knowing
  you can't pay for your sin?*

- *Sin was Adam's gift to mankind. What was
  Jesus' great gift?*

Apply:

You've just read a passage of the *great comparison*
that promised the *great exchange* to *great sinners*. The
comparison was the sin of the very first man and
Jesus' perfect sacrifice that paid for that sin. The great
exchange is the life of a sinner for a new life offered
by the One who rescues. The great sinners are those
who breathe. Jesus' lavish gift that could save mankind from their worst decisions brought certainty to
incredibly uncertain times.

You will need to be uncertain about your own choices before you can be certain that God's great rescue plan is a perfect fit. If you *think* this is an option you can take or leave, God described it as your only option when you need a new life and a fresh start.

He'll take care of the forgiveness and love you need. He'll even help you believe that what He says is true. He can remove uncertainty because He has done all the hard work.

Pray:

You said everyone sins. You said that no one can ever meet Your standards without help. You're the One who helps. You've never sinned, and You never will. You bring certain hope to uncertain days. I can find myself uncertain about so many things, but I want to be certain that You love me. Help me compare the benefits of Your love and exchange my past for Your future.

DEFIANT AND DEFLECTING
Read Genesis 4:1-16

Key Verse:

[God] said, "What have you done? The voice of your brother's blood cries out to Me from the ground."
GENESIS 4:10 NKJV

Understand:

- *Why might it be a bad idea to make decisions when you're angry?*

- *What does this passage say to you about the power of a parent's example?*

Apply:

Cain was angry, but he really didn't have a right to be. He made a choice to give something to God that God didn't want. When God honored his brother Abel but did not honor him, Cain lost it. Maybe he thought he was being creative or generous, but God knew that—more than just not listening—Cain made the wrong choice. Then, in his anger, Cain defiantly killed his brother.

Think about this: Cain was angry with God but killed his brother. Things don't make sense when you're angry. If he couldn't be angry with God, then he chose to deflect his anger toward the brother who was honored by God.

In his uncertain moment, Cain chose defiance as an ally. He didn't express a hint of remorse. What Cain did to Abel had never happened before—a human had never taken the life of a human. This uncertain moment would have ended differently if Cain had sought God instead of misguided revenge.

Pray:

I don't want to make life-changing decisions when I'm angry, Lord. You don't want me to make decisions when I'm upset. Help me stop assuming I have to retaliate when someone hurts me. Let me express remorse when I sin and refuse to blame someone else for my choices. I have been uncertain, and I will be again. I want to make choices that honor You and reflect this new life You've given me.

UNCERTAIN ON PURPOSE

Read Acts 9:1-19

Key Verse:

Now Saul, still breathing threats and murder against the disciples of the Lord, went to the high priest, and asked for letters from him to the synagogues at Damascus, so that if he found any belonging to the Way, both men and women, he might bring them bound to Jerusalem.

ACTS 9:1–2 NASB

Understand:

- *How has God gotten your attention when you've made wrong choices?*

- *How might it be possible for you to take action even when you are uncertain?*

Apply:

Saul had a pedigree. He had the right credentials. If he lived today, he might think of himself as a crime fighter or a spiritual superhero. He settled for learning about God without really knowing Him. That caused him to make choices that reflected wrong thinking instead of right action.

Saul held the coats of killers when Stephen, a follower of Jesus, was stoned to death. He threatened

Christians and said they would be killed. He was so certain he was right. He was a first-century vigilante.

Jesus made him intentionally uncertain. Saul had to question what he believed. Was he really as right in his thinking as he believed he was?

Then Saul was temporarily blinded by Jesus. This encounter (and condition) is why he became uncertain. It allowed Saul time to consider that he might have been wrong. Meeting Jesus changed defiance to remorse and a superiority complex to humility.

Pray:

When I'm feeling unsure, remind me that You ask me to slow down and think about what I'm doing. Uncertainty isn't always a bad thing, and uncertain times demand I spend time with You to learn the best way to respond. I will face plenty of uncertain times—help me to be certain that You can lead me through.

THAT MAKES NO SENSE
Read Genesis 6:9-22

Key Verse:

Noah did everything that God commanded him.
GENESIS 6:22 NCV

Understand:

- *Why is it hard to do what God asks when what He asks doesn't seem to match your personal interests?*

- *What is the only answer that will please God when He gives you a new assignment?*

Apply:

God probably hears more delayed answers than anything. It takes time to get used to the idea of obeying God. His plans seem time-consuming or outside your comfort zone. You might think He has asked the wrong person.

Imagine Noah. God gave him directions to build the first floating zoo. Admission was free, but no one took a tour. The boat was built to float even though Noah was nowhere near water for floating. His sons would need to help even when people made fun of their family.

If there was a recipe for uncertainty, then Noah knew the taste well. He obeyed God, but in those moments of obedience he was faced with hearing from neighbors who had no reason to believe Noah was of sound mind. What he was doing made no sense. Where he was building made no sense. The future flood he described was completely unknown.

When God asks you to do something that seems confusing, you should remember it only has to make sense to Him. God asked Noah to build an ark. At the right time God brought the water.

Pray:

I don't need to be uncertain when You've made the plans.
When Your plans are different than my experience,
then I should consider it an opportunity to go
on an adventure with Someone who already
knows the way. Uncertainty is normal,
but it doesn't have to be my first choice.

DESTRUCTION AVOIDANCE
Read Hebrews 2:1-9

Key Verse:

If we refuse this great way of being saved, how can we hope to escape? The Lord himself was the first to tell about it, and people who heard the message proved to us that it was true.
HEBREWS 2:3 CEV

Understand:

- *How might this passage remind you of Noah?*

- *Why should you take God's willingness to rescue seriously?*

Apply:

Jesus saves. You heard it. You believed it. Then? You didn't think so much about it. When you stop listening, you begin to drift away from the truth. God wants your full attention. It's time to show up, listen, and learn.

The Gospel is God's good news. His *good news* is that when you were lost and on a collision course with destruction, Jesus showed up and you were given the opportunity to redirect and discover life.

You were born into a world where personal destruction is the starting point. You won't get better, do better, or be better on your own. No one else will either. There's one way to find rescue, and you can't rescue yourself.

God made a plan to save humans, yet when Jesus came, people laughed and made fun of Him. They didn't see Him as the Great Rescuer. They certainly didn't see Him as the only rescue plan they would ever need.

Pray:

You're the great surprise, Lord Jesus. You have plans I never expect that result in a life You call abundant. You give me a purpose and a hope, and then You invite me on the adventure of my life. I could spend time and energy thinking about why following You doesn't make sense, or I could follow and watch You save me from being destroyed. Following—that's my choice.

UNCERTAINTY THROUGH CONFUSION

Read Genesis 11:1–9

Key Verse:

[The LORD said,] "Come, let us go down and confuse their language so they will not understand each other."
GENESIS 11:7 NIV

Understand:

- *Why is it easy to be uncertain when you are going through a time of confusion?*

- *How can God use times of confusion to bring you closer to Him?*

Apply:

You're aware of someone who knows everything and he's willing to PowerPoint. Or one who believes her family name is Knowitall, and she's a proud branch on the family tree. When they show up, others find a reason to leave. You're certain these individuals know something—even if it's just how to annoy. They are like ants at a family picnic, the anxious neighbor dog at midnight, or the neighbor whose favorite topics are things you've never heard of before.

Sometimes when you think you're smarter than most, God will take your pride and redirect it in ways you struggle to make sense of. He did that for a group of people who thought they were smarter than Him. They believed that if they could just build a tower tall enough, then they could reach heaven and become famous for finding God through sheer cleverness.

God knew the people could get closer to Him if they kept their feet on the ground. Uncertainty provided the people with a reason to rediscover the Famous One.

Pray:

When I'm confused and not at all certain, help me remember to stop looking for answers in places where You haven't been welcome. In my most recent uncertainty, shut off all escape routes except the one that leads to You. Help me understand that I will always be more uncertain when I choose not to walk with You.

A MENTAL DINNER PARTY
Read Philippians 4:4-9

Key Verse:

*Fix your thoughts on what is true, and honorable,
and right, and pure, and lovely, and admirable. Think
about things that are excellent and worthy of praise.*
PHILIPPIANS 4:8 NLT

Understand:

- *What are some benefits of putting barriers
  around what you think?*

- *How can thought barriers lead you to a place
  of joy?*

Apply:

Your mind will think even when you don't want it
to. You could send unproductive, unwelcome, and
unwise thoughts on a one-way trip out of your mind
or throw them a dinner party. If you choose the
dinner party, you can expect those thoughts to make
themselves long-term mental guests. They won't
leave on their own.

Establish some house rules for a productive
thought life. When a thought drops by, ask whether

it's true or a lie. If it's a lie, don't wait; politely but firmly send it on. Is it honorable or immoral? Is it pure or counterfeit? Is it lovely or disagreeable? Is it admirable or repulsive? Is it excellent or inappropriate? Is it worthy of praise or rebuke? Your answers to these questions will mean the difference between faith and uncertainty, joy and despair, hope and fear.

Give your thoughts some godly guidance. Give fruitless thinking a mental fast. Others will notice your change in thinking.

Pray:

My mind can invite me on an unapproved journey, but I don't have to go. I can be certain that You've given me everything I need to focus my thoughts on things that remind me of You. Guard my mind. Help me make thought choices that please You. And when I let my mind stay in a place You've marked as off-limits, help me admit my wrong choice and come face-to-face with forgiveness.

ADDRESS CHANGE

Read Genesis 12:1-9

Key Verse:

Now the LORD had said to Abram: "Get out of your country, from your family and from your father's house, to a land that I will show you."

GENESIS 12:1 NKJV

Understand:

- *Why does moving seem to make you more vulnerable to uncertainty?*

- *Why is it hard to trust God's plan even when you're convinced it's what He wants for you?*

Apply:

You're moving, but you're not sure you're ready for the disconnection of utilities, final bills for the place you're leaving, and the sense of unknown between *here and familiar* and *there and uncertain*.

Friends and extended family may be left behind for future friends who are yet undiscovered. Sometimes you plan for the new chapter, but there's still a lot you have to overcome once you fill out a change of address form.

Abram got the call. He was being transferred. Was it good news? Bad news? The best news was that God gave Abram directions and made a few promises.

This was the great restart, a new chapter, a blank slate. At seventy-five, Abram was asked to begin something new when most people were staying where they were, believing there was little more to their story. Be certain of this—sometimes God asks you to move.

Pray:

Before You ever ask me to move, You invite me to follow. I must be willing to take steps in Your direction before I'm commissioned to adventure. There's life after unloading a moving truck. And since You're the Author of my faith, You write the story before, during, and after the move. The challenges I face don't surprise You, and You can take care of each challenge. I don't have to know how You're going to help to know that You will.

THE RETURN OF
OLD MISTAKES

Read Mark 10:17–27

Key Verse:

*Jesus felt a love for [the rich man] and said to
him, "One thing you lack: go and sell all you
possess and give to the poor, and you will have
treasure in heaven; and come, follow Me."*

MARK 10:21 NASB

Understand:

- *Why was the rich man comfortable just
  following the rules?*

- *What was the importance of having
  compassion and following Jesus?*

Apply:

Sometimes people follow God at a distance and on
their own terms. That was the case with the rich
man. He was a good man. He followed the rules.
He wanted to impress. But when Jesus asked him
to vacate his comfort zone, his actions said, "No
thanks."

Like Abram, this man was asked to leave the

familiar for something new, but he just couldn't do it. He liked being among the best at following the rules. He just didn't have time to follow Jesus *and* show compassion to people. As long as the rich man could justify his own actions, there wasn't a need for change.

Feeling uncertain often means returning to old mistakes. Bravery is thought to be for someone younger or with fewer entanglements. Uncertainty sits out the dance, forgoes the ride, and waves off the wonder. Faith, in contrast, says it pays to be bold.

Pray:

Today You ask me to follow You. It doesn't matter whether I've been a lifelong rule follower or have been on a lawbreaking binge. You invite me to follow. I can decline Your offer because I think I'm not such a bad person, or I can decline because I think I have to be better first. Your qualification for following is. . . to follow. Uncertainty has multiple sources. Forgiveness comes from One. Help me to follow You and accept Your forgiveness—no waiting.

NO KIDDING
Read Genesis 18:1-15

Key Verse:

Abraham and Sarah were very old. Since Sarah was past the age when women normally have children, she laughed to herself, "My husband and I are too old to have a baby."
GENESIS 18:11–12 NCV

Understand:

- *How do you think you'd respond if God arrived for a visit?*

- *What makes it so hard to believe something is yours if you have to wait for it for a very long time?*

Apply:

The original postmark reads "September 21, 1996." A lot of time has passed since it was sent on a journey to you, but it hasn't arrived. You've thought for years that it was lost in the mail. You stopped waiting for it. Then you receive an email letting you know it will be delivered soon, but you've heard that before—and think you'll be left waiting again.

Don't be too hard on Sarah. This was the struggle she faced when God said that His promise was coming true. She laughed. It seemed incredible, too good to be true. Maybe she felt it was too late. It certainly left her uncertain about what to believe.

Feeling confused and conflicted is normal with uncertainty. Faith asks you to believe when you live in the middle of *all things uncertain*.

Pray:

I can read Your Word and know that Sarah had a child. I can know an entire nation came from the birth of that child. I can even chalk it up to Your promises. I have proof that You are good and answer prayers. I've read it. But Sarah lived it. She didn't have the benefit of knowing how things would turn out. She expressed human uncertainty. Help me use this truth to maintain the status of one who trusts.

THE DEAD USUALLY STAY DEAD

Read John 20:24-29

Key Verse:

Thomas said, "First, I must see the nail scars in his hands and touch them with my finger. I must put my hand where the spear went into his side. I won't believe unless I do this!"

JOHN 20:25 CEV

Understand:

- *What are some of the similarities and differences between Thomas and Sarah?*

- *How can you identify with the uncertainty experienced by Thomas?*

Apply:

Thomas saw Jesus, served Jesus, and was saved by Jesus. He was a disciple and he was all in. The truth was out—*Jesus was crucified.* The proof was in—*He was placed in a tomb.* But then the other disciples said, "We have seen the Lord!" (John 20:25 CEV).

Thomas was logical, practical, sensible. He'd never heard of anyone rising from the dead. He was risking his sanity, knowing that 100 percent of the people he knew who died *stayed dead*. Sure, there was the time Jesus called Lazarus from the dead, but could Jesus rise from the dead on His own? Thomas spoke fluent uncertainty.

Then Thomas was invited to inspect the impossible. Jesus asked him to look at the places where He was wounded. It took a little while for Thomas to move his mind from thinking Jesus' resurrection was logically impossible to accepting it as a certain fact. Soon, though, disbelief was replaced by faith.

Pray:

There are times when I can be where Thomas was.
Help me make the same move in Your direction.
I can learn from Sarah and Thomas that You're always
more than I think, that Your promises are truer than
my faith. Your plan doesn't always make sense in the
middle of trust, but it makes perfect sense in hindsight.
Turn my doubts to certainty. Help me remember
that trusting You really does make sense.

MELANCHOLY MORNING
Read Genesis 22:1-18

Key Verse:

"Do not lay a hand on the boy," [the angel of the
Lord] said. "Do not do anything to him. Now
I know that you fear God, because you have not
withheld from me your son, your only son."
GENESIS 22:12 NIV

Understand:

- *How do you feel when it seems God asks too*
  much of you?

- *What kinds of tests have you gone through?*
  Did God help?

Apply:

It was just a morning stroll, or was it? One melancholy man and his son would end up at Mount Moriah. It must have been a rather silent journey. Abraham had a lot to think about, and the son wrestled with the uncertainty of one who knows something important is happening but isn't sure what.

The boy carried wood for a sacrifice while the father carried instructions that were soul crushing: "Take your son, your only son, whom you love—Isaac—and go to the region of Moriah. Sacrifice him there" (Genesis 22:2 NIV). God had said this boy would be the start of a great nation. Had Abraham done something to make God change His mind?

Abraham's aging eyes took in the vitality of the young boy Isaac. Each footstep led them closer to a makeshift mountain altar.

When Abraham was certain there was no other way, God made a way. There would be a sacrifice, but God offered a substitute.

Pray:

I can't always understand why You test me, Lord, but I'm better for enduring tests that stretch my faith and try my patience. I'm not You and I'm not allowed to see the end result, but each challenge leads me to the wisdom that stories of Your faithfulness are at the end of my personal stories. Help me share Your faithfulness.

THE CURE

Read 1 John 4:7-18

Key Verse:

God showed how much he loved us by sending his one and only Son into the world so that we might have eternal life through him.

1 JOHN 4:9 NLT

Understand:

- *With whom does love originate?*
- *What proof do you have that God loves you?*

Apply:

Spoiler alert: Love was God's great cure for uncertainty. In today's passage this cure is mentioned nearly two dozen times. It's hard to miss, yet it is often overlooked and misunderstood.

This cure has a companion promise that leaves you in the company of God forever.

God walked with His only Son through life on earth. His Son would establish the mightiest kingdom that would ever be known. Moments became days that took their place in a story of years. A mob chanted, leaders mobilized against God's Son, and crude spikes held Jesus to executioner's beams. There was no need for a substitute this time because Jesus *was* your substitute. Your sin demanded death as payment, and Jesus effectively said, "I can satisfy your debt, and I will." You might cringe at the picture of His death, but He endured this violence once and it was enough for all time—and for all people who are willing to trade uncertainty for His love.

Pray:

Uncertainty thrives in a courtroom. So much is unknown and so much is on the line. Freedom can be lost at a moment's notice, and a guilty verdict gives uncertainty extra strength. Yet I don't have the same response when I have a conversation with a friend. When I'm judged I know I'm guilty enough to be condemned, but when I'm loved I'm accepted enough to believe in second chances and a future that could be different than my past.

THE COVER-UP
Read Genesis 37:12-28

Key Verse:

"Come therefore, let us now kill him and cast him into some pit; and we shall say, 'Some wild beast has devoured him.' We shall see what will become of his dreams!"
GENESIS 37:20 NKJV

Understand:

- *Why should sin leave you uncertain?*
- *Why can't an injustice cancel an injustice?*

Apply:

It must have been easy to be jealous of Joseph. Who could blame his older brothers for wanting him to be quiet? After all, he'd been the one to claim they would one day worship him. He was the one who received a coat from Dad that screamed, "I'm Dad's favorite."

He stayed home while his brothers worked. He shared dreams while they only had stories of sheep. They were certain this *kid* had done them wrong. They wanted to teach him a lesson but didn't want to get in trouble with Dad.

When Joseph came to them alone, they plotted to kill him and then sold him into slavery and then agreed to lie about it.

Sin wants you to invite its entire family over. One sin becomes two and two become a dozen. Soon you have more sin to feed than you can afford, but to send them away means you have to agree that God is right and you were wrong. Welcome to uncertainty's struggle.

Pray:

There's no such thing as a white lie, Lord, so keep me from convincing myself that some sin isn't so bad. I can sin and then sin again to cover it up. I can lose track of how many times and all of the ways I have offended You. Help me remember that a right relationship with You should be my preference when the confusion of sin leaves me uncertain.

PERSONALLY EXCUSED SIN

Read John 8:31-47

Key Verse:

[Jesus said,] "If I speak truth, why do you not believe Me? He who is of God hears the words of God; for this reason you do not hear them, because you are not of God."
John 8:46–47 NASB

Understand:

- *Why is it easy for people to struggle to believe Jesus?*

- *How can people redefine injustice and make it sound like justice?*

Apply:

Who would side with the one-man opposition? It was Jesus standing against all the religious leaders, and they didn't agree with Him. He told the truth, and they said it was a lie. He said He knew God, and they said it was impossible. When some seemed to believe, Jesus said, "If you continue in My word, then you are truly disciples of Mine; and you will know the truth, and the truth will make you free" (John 8:31–32 NASB).

Herd mentality swayed belief to uncertainty. A new majority was formed, but the majority was wrong. The religious leaders were playing a multiplication game with sin, and they couldn't see how big they were losing.

The people excused their own sin or chose to call it by a name that sounded more noble. They were in the presence of God's Son and in a very real sense called Him a liar. It had happened before. It still happens.

Pray:

Your laws, promises, and plans are not to be dismissed because I don't like what they say about me or the world around me. I will never look, act, or sound more like You than when I agree that living in the middle of what You call truth is the only real choice that pleases You. Help me see You as the source for truth and the place where hope is born. I want to be certain that You are truth.

A CHANGE IN CIRCUMSTANCE

Read Genesis 41:14-41

Key Verse:

*"People will forget what it was like to have plenty of
food, because the hunger that follows will be so great.
You had two dreams which mean the same thing.
This shows that God has firmly decided that this will
happen, and he will make it happen soon."*

GENESIS 41:31–32 NCV

Understand:

- *Why do you think God made part of His
  plan known to the king through Joseph?*

- *How did this information change the
  direction of Joseph's life?*

Apply:

Joseph, the former favored son and falsely accused
slave, spent some time in prison. That was before the
king asked Joseph for help. The king had two dreams,
and he was uncertain what they meant.

No one had listed a personal ad for a dream
interpreter, but when Joseph helped a man with

dream interpretation, the king eventually found out and Joseph was brought out from prison. He gave God the credit and then listened to the dreams. He told the king a famine was coming and he should get prepared.

The king trusted Joseph's interpretation. Because the king was still a bit uncertain, he hired a prisoner to be his second in command.

Wisdom adds perspective to uncertainty. That wisdom comes from God's Word. The truth of God's Word dislodges uncertainty.

Pray:

*You can do anything at any time for anyone.
The circumstances I face today may not be the plot
or setting for my future. When I live in uncertain times,
help me remember the time you changed the future of
a prisoner in Egypt who followed You. I will live
in uncertain times with the certainty that I am
not forgotten or abandoned by You. The love You
have for me will lead me to You every time.*

A PLAN TO RESCUE ANYONE

Read Acts 10:9-35

Key Verse:

*Peter said to them, "You know that we Jews are
not allowed to have anything to do with other people.
But God has shown me that he doesn't think
anyone is unclean or unfit."*
ACTS 10:28 CEV

Understand:

- *What does this passage suggest about a
  relationship with God?*

- *Why was it hard for Peter to accept this
  truth from God?*

Apply:

It was a dream or maybe a vision that Peter struggled
to understand. God showed him all kinds of animals
and asked him to find something to eat. Peter had
followed a strict Jewish diet and couldn't find anything that would have been on his regular menu.
Peter turned God down. God made the offer three
times. Sometimes we need a little help to understand
what God is saying.

More than making a statement about food, God

was letting Peter know that He had a plan to rescue anyone. Peter would go on to say, "God is pleased with everyone who worships him and does right, no matter what nation they come from" (Acts 10:35 cev). Peter's vision was a reminder that God was willing to accept anyone who followed Him. No one was off the list. No one was unwelcome.

God was preparing Peter to preach a message to people who were uncertain if they were welcome.

Pray:

*Peter seemed to need a lot of reminders of Your love.
So do I. When You have a message to share, You've always
worked to ensure that people can understand it. That's why
You've given us the Bible. Nothing it says is a wasted read.
Help me read it, believe it, and then share it. Even when
I don't understand other people, help me remember
that Your love for them is never diminished
by what I don't know.*

LIFE AND THE WORDS THAT HEAL

Read Genesis 45:4-28

Key Verse:

[Joseph said,] "God sent me ahead of you to preserve for you a remnant on earth and to save your lives by a great deliverance."
GENESIS 45:7 NIV

Understand:

- *What surprises you most about Joseph's response to his brothers?*

- *How can your responses decrease the level of uncertainty for others?*

Apply:

Maybe you've heard the phrase, "Speak life into others." It sounds good but is not always easily understood. There may be other meanings, but many use this phrase to say that they want to encourage others in a way that makes them bold and courageous.

Take Joseph—he came face-to-face with the brothers who had wanted to kill him. These were the brothers who sold him into slavery and made it impossible for him to see his younger brother or dad. No one would have been surprised if he was angry with them, but Joseph chose to speak life into his brothers. He chose to honor God for arranging circumstances he hadn't understood to save a bunch of sinners. *Sound familiar?*

Joseph's response was unexpected. It brought a family together. It served to heal old wounds. Your response to a difficult situation can make people uncertain, but maybe it doesn't need to.

Pray:

Sometimes I want to tell people exactly what I think about them. I want them to know that they hurt me and that I have no intention of forgiving them. Somehow I think it will help make me feel better, but it never does. Maybe that's why forgiveness is tied so closely to love and love is tied so closely to certainty. Help me take Your words and use them to help me speak life—even to those who've hurt me.

A FISHERMAN'S
FORGIVEN FAILINGS

Read John 21:1-17

Key Verse:

At dawn Jesus was standing on the beach,
but the disciples couldn't see who he was.
JOHN 21:4 NLT

Understand:

- *Before he was a disciple, Peter was a*
  fisherman. Why might that be important to
  this event?

- *Peter denied that he knew Jesus. Why was*
  restoration needed?

Apply:

Peter would line up to be the first to try really big things, but follow-through was not a skill he'd developed. He wanted to walk on water with Jesus but started to sink when he became uncertain. He said he was willing to die with Jesus but ran away when that looked like a real possibility.

After Jesus rose from the dead, Peter saw the man he had run away from. He saw the man who had shared the water when he was invited to walk on the waves. Jesus was on the beach and Peter was in a boat. For a moment he forgot his failings, threw himself in the water, and swam to shore.

Jesus needed to talk to the fisherman who seemed to have forgotten he was a disciple. Peter needed a reason to believe he could still be useful. Jesus spoke life into Peter three different ways. Peter never heard Him say, "Catch My fish." He heard, "Take care of My sheep."

Pray:

Why is it so easy to help people remember their faults? Maybe I don't think they remember. But they usually do, and my words don't seem to help. Your example tells me that You don't want to leave me uncertain about how You feel about me and that Your love can take me from where I am to a place that looks a lot like Your plan. Help me give and accept encouragement.

A COMMON UNCERTAINTY

Read Exodus 1:8-22

Key Verse:

Now there arose a new king over Egypt,
who did not know Joseph.
Exodus 1:8 nkjv

Understand:

- *Why does a new set of life circumstances leave you feeling uncertain?*

- *When you are the most uncertain, what are a few of the thoughts you often think?*

Apply:

When God takes you through one trouble, you can be sure He can do it again—and again.

If there were a tracking program for early history, then you'd see that God showed up for Adam and Eve, Noah, Abraham, Isaac, Jacob, Joseph, and more. Today's passage suggests a lot of people were looking for delivery from trouble. They lived in the city of Uncertainty and were told they couldn't leave.

They had been guests but found themselves in the role of slaves. The work was harder than it needed to be, the conditions were harsher than anyone expected, and babies were given a death sentence.

God had a plan and He was certain that this group of people would be free again, but first the man He would use to rescue the people would need to be born. That's a story for another study.

Pray:

I can think about the worst thing I have ever lived through and discover that someone has lived through something worse. That means I can understand the uncertainty that other people feel. I can remember what bad days are like. But I can also remember Your faithfulness. I can remember that uncertainty doesn't have to be permanent. Help me show kindness and help others whenever possible, because so many people are wondering if being uncertain is their new normal. You say it doesn't have to be.

UNCOMFORTABLE TRUTH

Read Acts 7:44-60

Key Verse:

They cried out with a loud voice, and covered their ears and rushed at him with one impulse. When they had driven him out of the city, they began stoning him.
ACTS 7:57–58 NASB

Understand:

- *Why do you feel uncertain when you are misunderstood?*

- *Can you think of a time when something good came from something bad? Describe it.*

Apply:

It might have been unplanned, but Stephen found himself teaching a history lesson to those who were uncomfortable with his conclusions. Stephen suggested that Moses understood communication with God much more than the religious leaders who were listening to him speak. They came from a long line of people who refused to believe the messenger prophets whom God had sent to tell them *uncomfortable truth*. They hated feeling uncertain so they usually tried to stop these men from speaking. These religious leaders observed behavior they then modeled for their own families, and Stephen called them "stiff-necked." They didn't like his description.

And like the Egyptian king, the leaders sought to punish the messenger. Like the king, the leaders were scared and uncertain. Like the king, the leaders didn't stop at making one bad choice.

God made you to be part of His family. He made you to love others. You can do that with His help.

Pray:

You want me to speak words that are true, Lord.
You want me to speak words that demonstrate Your love.
When I combine these two—truth and love—uncertainty
becomes less powerful. This is true for others, and it is
absolutely true for me. Help me follow You when it's
hard, honor You when others think it's strange,
and love others because You loved me first.

POSITION OF LAST RESORT

Read Exodus 2:1-10

Key Verse:

The king's daughter opened the basket and saw the baby boy. He was crying, so she felt sorry for him and said, "This is one of the Hebrew babies."
EXODUS 2:6 NCV

Understand:

- *Why can family dynamics leave you uncertain?*

- *How can unfulfilled plans leave you confused?*

Apply:

A defenseless baby lay in a small makeshift boat. He was in the position of last resort. When he was born there was a law that made the killing of baby boys lawful and the refusal to kill them criminal. But Moses *was* born, and no one had killed him in those minutes after his first cry. His parents hid him. Perhaps they hoped the law would change. They were waiting on a miracle. This predicament left them uncertain.

So the infant floated while his sister watched. He was too big to hide very well. That's when the king's daughter came to the river. She spotted the floating basket and looked inside. This was the day a member of Egyptian royalty adopted a boy who was supposed to have been killed. God brought a miracle through someone most thought of as an enemy.

This was the boy God would train to become the man used to deliver His people from Egypt, but for forty years Moses was raised as an Egyptian. Even still, God was his Instructor.

Pray:

When the thing I want most doesn't happen, help me remember this story. Sometimes Your greatest blessings don't feel that way at all. I want to understand that You know the outcome of every trial and You can bring a miracle to the most desperate situation. I can turn down every potential miracle by simply refusing to follow. Help me choose obedience instead.

GOD DELIVERED

Read Romans 6:8–23

Key Verse:

When you were slaves of sin, you didn't have to please God. But what good did you receive from the things you did?
ROMANS 6:20–21 CEV

Understand:

- *What is the importance of being delivered?*
- *How can deliverance improve certainty?*

Apply:

Jesus came to give slaves freedom. That's especially good news, but former slaves can be comfortable with the normalcy of slavery. It might be easier to say yes to sin because it has been pretty bossy for most of your life. Following God can make you feel uncertain because it's hard to do what God wants you to do when it doesn't bear a resemblance to answering the call of your former slave identity. Uncertainty brought about by God, however, can motivate you to change course.

You were delivered from sin, so your freedom is not to conduct business as usual but to embrace a new life that recognizes a new way to live, act, and think. Don't expect things to change overnight. God has always been aware that people who were born as sinners will sin, but your thinking began to change the moment uncertainty led you to the God who delivers. Where you've been becomes less enticing the more you learn about where you're going.

Pray:

I'm never left to figure things out on my own. You make sure I have Your help. I'm never left to feel unloved. You sent Jesus to show me how much You love me. I'm never left to learn alone. Your Spirit is my Teacher. You've given me three powerful reasons to put my uncertain circumstances in Your strong hands. Help me let You take care of them.

TO SERVE A PURPOSE

Read Exodus 2:11-25

Key Verse:

The king of Egypt died. The Israelites groaned in their slavery and cried out, and their cry for help because of their slavery went up to God. God heard their groaning and he remembered his covenant.
EXODUS 2:23–24 NIV

Understand:

- *Do you think God ever forgets to be faithful? Why or why not?*

- *Why does uncertainty show up before certainty does?*

Apply:

Moses ran away from Egypt. He thought he was helping his family, but it wasn't long before public opinion shifted and Moses was on the run. For more than three decades he'd been an adopted son in the palace. He had everything he wanted, but he had to face uncertainty before God could use him.

In this time of uncertainty Moses met his wife, watched his children grow, and lived the life of a humble shepherd. And while he was living a quiet life, God saw that His people needed a deliverer. It was nearly time for Moses to face an even greater sense of bewilderment.

Maybe Moses thought the best there would ever be was somewhere in his past. Perhaps he thought he had messed things up enough that this wilderness retreat was all he could hope for. There's little evidence that Moses had any idea what God had in mind. You don't either, but He promises a good plan. He says it will serve a purpose.

Pray:

Sometimes I feel set aside without purpose. I don't know what to do, and I feel like I've done nothing useful or important. Help me understand that You may be preparing me for something unexpected. Help me understand that my uncertainty can be replaced by Your love. My fear can leave when I begin to trust You.

SUCH SORROW

Read Matthew 26:36-46

Key Verse:

*[Jesus] told them, "My soul is crushed with grief to the
point of death. Stay here and keep watch with me."*
MATTHEW 26:38 NLT

Understand:

- *Why is it important to remember that Jesus
  experienced grief?*

- *How can prayer bridge the gap between
  uncertainty and trust?*

Apply:

You would think that if you heard God's Son say that
He was experiencing soul-crushing grief, it might
leave you uncertain and several shades of nervous.
Not so with Peter, James, and John. They might have
been concerned as Jesus prayed with such sorrow,
but sleep was easier to understand and it had fewer
requirements.

They had just had a good meal, it was dark
outside, and sleep was a companion to those who
called Jesus their friend. Jesus asked the disciples to

pray *with* Him, not just try to watch Him pray. He wanted to be in the company of friends, but they wanted naptime.

The disciples didn't understand what Jesus would be going through, even though He told them. At the very least, they didn't believe anything would happen that night.

Prayer is the anytime, every time, all-the-time solution to the things you face. It keeps you in contact with the God who knows what happens next—and can help you get there.

Pray:

*You invite me to pray about things that You care about,
and sometimes I wait, sleep, or pass up the offer. You ask
me to join You in something bigger than me, and I wonder
if there's a show I could watch on TV instead. When I do
and uncertainty stays for the day, help me remember
Your offer and turn off the uncertainty.*

MY EXCUSES, HIS RESOURCES

Read Exodus 3:1–14

Key Verse:

*Moses said to God, "Who am I that I should
go to Pharaoh, and that I should bring the
children of Israel out of Egypt?"*
EXODUS 3:11 NKJV

Understand:

- *Why can you view excuses as either pride or
  selfishness?*

- *When should you accept God's plans? Why?*

Apply:

Moses was quick to tell God, "You've got the wrong
guy." He didn't immediately accept his mission. He
was filled with excuses. God's plan seemed the origin
of a legend, not something a flesh-and-bone man like
himself could accomplish. Moses? From introverted
wilderness dweller to national deliverer? Hadn't he
run away? Hadn't he made mistakes? Hadn't he
totally skipped being a slave in Egypt? It didn't matter. God said, "Go." There was no excuse that could

change His mind. No plea that got Moses off the hook. No logic that could defeat God's wisdom.

And who sent Moses? The God who always has been and always will be. The One described as the Great I Am. The One who has more resources than you have excuses. He is the One who can call you, prepare you, and send you. When you need help, He'll help you. He may even send others to help you. Don't let fear stop you from accepting God's assignments.

Pray:

I can find all kinds of reasons to believe that anyone else would be a better choice to help You than me. I can point out my sin, my unfaithfulness to You, and my bent toward selfishness, but when You call, it's not a mistake. You can work through my uncertainty and uncertain times to forge a way when no one saw it coming. Help me agree to Your two-step process—You lead; I'll follow.

MEDIATING UNCERTAINTY

Read Philemon 1:1–21

Key Verse:

For perhaps [Onesimus] was for this reason separated from you for a while, that you would have him back forever, no longer as a slave, but more than a slave, a beloved brother, especially to me, but how much more to you, both in the flesh and in the Lord.

Philemon 1:15–16 NASB

Understand:

- *How does unforgiveness hurt relationships?*

- *Why might you need help in restoring a broken relationship?*

Apply:

Two men experiencing the great divide. Onesimus wronged Philemon. Philemon wasn't in the mood to forgive Onesimus. It almost seemed like it was high noon and the duo faced each other with no one willing to budge. That's when Onesimus ran and Philemon grabbed a bottle of bitterness.

Someone needed to mediate this state of uncertainty. That man was Paul. He recognized that both men had changed. Onesimus had taken responsibility for his actions. Philemon had taken a "no forgiveness" stance. That made it hard for Onesimus to make things right.

Stubbornness can sometimes lengthen the days of dilemma. Stubbornness leaves everyone at a stoplight that never changes. You can't go forward, and there's no room to back up.

God can send good friends who can help you remember that God forgave you and equipped you to love others. He can also take your unfaithfulness and exchange it for usefulness. He did that for Onesimus. He can do it for you.

Pray:

You want me to forgive for a lot of reasons, but maybe one of the best reasons is it helps me rediscover friendship. It keeps me from being isolated and alone. Too often I am confused, believing everyone is against me, but when You are for me, no one can really stand against me.

AN APPOINTMENT WITH GOD

Read Exodus 4:1–17

Key Verse:

Then the LORD said to [Moses], "Who made a person's mouth? And who makes someone deaf or not able to speak? Or who gives a person sight or blindness? It is I, the LORD. Now go! I will help you speak, and I will teach you what to say."
EXODUS 4:11–12 NCV

Understand:

- *Who made your mouth? What words should you say?*

- *Why is it unwise to believe God might be confused?*

Apply:

You have an appointment with God. You've never heard Him speak before. You're awestruck when you meet Him, and you're listening carefully to what He says. He has an important assignment, and you're honored that He'd ask. But the assignment is overwhelming, and you object, saying you can't speak well. Before you can utter another word, God responds: "Who made a person's mouth? And who makes someone deaf or not able to speak? Or who gives a person sight or blindness? It is I, the LORD. Now go!"

That should be enough to convince anyone to go, but it wasn't for Moses—and it might not be for you. This was an uncertain time in his life. It might be like asking a rancher to head to the big city to talk to a world leader. Moses would be the deliverer; he just needed to move past himself to the God who has never been uncertain.

Pray:

I want to think beyond myself to what You can do. I want to live in the middle of Your adventure and hold tightly to the "better than a bucket list" moments with Your Spirit. I can't do that when I either tell You no or suggest I can't do what You tell me I can—with Your help.

NO ROOM FOR DOUBT

Read Matthew 28:11-20

Key Verse:

[Jesus said,] "Go to the people of all nations and make them my disciples."
MATTHEW 28:19 CEV

Understand:

- *What do using your mouth and being certain have in common?*

- *What role does obedience play in being certain?*

Apply:

Unlike Moses, the disciples had spent as many as three years sitting under the teaching of God's Son. They'd heard about and seen His miracles and wisdom and the profound ways He affected people's lives. Jesus was clear about what He would do. He shared freely about what they should do. But it's interesting that just before Jesus gave His great assignment after rising from the dead, the Bible discloses one Moses-inspired note: "Some of them doubted" (Matthew 28:17 CEV).

Jesus said He would rise from the dead, yet some of them doubted. Would they also doubt His simple but powerful message to take what they knew and help others follow Jesus the way they did? They were told to tell others and never stop. They were told to go and keep going. This assignment was huge, but first they had to believe that what Jesus said was true. They couldn't doubt that He rose from the dead and that He was God's Son. He could give them the words to speak and the strength to live life the way He wanted them to live.

Pray:

It's so easy to be a skeptic. I can accept truth when I see it in action, but faith is trusting You and believing that You are with me. You don't leave me alone, but You might ask me to do more than I think I can because You plan to help. So walk with me as I talk with You. Remind me I'm not alone and I never have been.

GOD IS PATIENT

Read Exodus 5:1-23

Key Verse:

Moses returned to the LORD and said, "Why, Lord, why have you brought trouble on this people? Is this why you sent me? Ever since I went to Pharaoh to speak in your name, he has brought trouble on this people, and you have not rescued your people at all."
EXODUS 5:22–23 NIV

Understand:

- *Why do people want to believe that bad things never happen to good people?*

- *How does this part of Moses' story challenge this idea?*

Apply:

An uncertain Moses left the more certain comfort of his wilderness home. God had overcome his objections, and the runaway returned to the home of his youth. Things were different. The king was different. The circumstances? *Not so much.*

Maybe Moses thought he would meet the king, prove God was strong, and then watch the king give up. *That didn't happen.* Moses might have wondered what he'd gotten himself into. The man who had said he had trouble speaking suddenly found a way to tell God exactly what was on his mind. Like Adam before him, Moses pulled out the blame game, and his opponent was God. It seemed Moses' motto was, "If at first you don't succeed, give up and criticize God." Thankfully God is patient with the uncertain. He is patient with you.

Pray:

When things don't turn out the way I think they should, it's easy to think that You could have done something about it but didn't. It's hard not knowing the end of the story yet living through plot twists that leave me questioning. But I'm seeing that You can be trusted with my entire story. I pray that You would be honored through my life, Lord.

STATE OF TROUBLE

Read Acts 5:17-42

Key Verse:

*The apostles left the high council rejoicing that
God had counted them worthy to suffer
disgrace for the name of Jesus.*
ACTS 5:41 NLT

Understand:

- *Why should people who follow God expect
  trouble?*

- *Should knowing that trouble is common
  leave you uncertain? Why or why not?*

Apply:

They were jealous men with the power to arrest. That combination meant that those who followed Jesus lived in an ongoing state of trouble. In this passage the opponents are clear. There are the religious leaders who despised Christians, and there are the Christians who believed in Jesus so much that they had to speak up—even when circumstances suggested they should be quiet.

One religious leader, however, gave some great

advice to his peers. Gamaliel saw the other religious leaders becoming very angry because news of Jesus was spreading. He told those leaders, "Leave these men alone. Let them go. If they are planning and doing these things merely on their own, it will soon be overthrown. But if it is from God, you will not be able to overthrow them. You may even find yourselves fighting against God!" (Acts 5:38–39 NLT).

Gamaliel didn't know the end of the story, but he knew that God had a history of doing the unexpected in a way that helped uncertain people living in uncertain times trust Him. He didn't want to be on the wrong side of God's plan.

Pray:

No one wants trouble. No one wants to think that their steps into the future are unclear. I want to remember that Your plan doesn't leave You uncomfortable. It gives me an opportunity to trust, which is what faith is all about. Help me be brave enough to walk with You and share what I'm learning.

THE GOD CHEER

Read Exodus 14:5-18

Key Verse:

Moses said to the people, "Do not be afraid.
Stand still, and see the salvation of the LORD,
which He will accomplish for you today."
EXODUS 14:13 NKJV

Understand:

- *Why do you need reminders that you should not be afraid?*

- *How can it help to read stories of God's faithfulness?*

Apply:

Moses was an aging man who was learning to grow up. Doubt switched places with trust, and in the bull's-eye of belief, hard questions were answered. Moses watched God make ten promises and keep every one. When the king of Egypt no longer wanted God to make promises, he gave the people of Israel an eviction notice. Pharaoh wanted the people gone. His stubbornness had done nothing to help his own people, and it would take awhile to recover.

When a newly freed nation of people reached the Red Sea, so did a message that reintroduced uncertainty. Pharaoh had changed his mind and sent soldiers to bring the people back. His plan was to snatch hope away from the hopeful. *That wasn't God's plan.*

Now, instead of Moses living the life of the uncertain, he chose to embrace belief. He gave a pep rally; he raised a *God cheer*; he used the mouth he thought was useless to speak words that encouraged. Something had changed for Moses—and God was the One who offered the change. The people were free, but they were far from home.

Pray:

When I enter Your company, I no longer need the company of confusion. When I trust You, I become bold. When I choose to walk with You, I become confident in Your leadership. Help me make the choices that invite faith so I can grow up in You.

CERTAIN WORSHIP
Read John 12:1-8

Key Verse:

Mary then took a pound of very costly perfume of pure nard, and anointed the feet of Jesus and wiped His feet with her hair; and the house was filled with the fragrance of the perfume.
JOHN 12:3 NASB

Understand:

- *Would you describe Mary's gift as an act of worship? Why or why not?*

- *Why would you need to be "certain" to offer a gift like Mary did?*

Apply:

Feel free to call worship "God cheer." God is worth saying good things about. He's worth songs of honor. He's worth your choice to praise. Some people might think your God cheer is too much, too often, or too lavish.

Today's passage describes this kind of worship. Mary had been following Jesus. She saw worth in the Son of God when others were unsure. She demonstrated honor when she washed His feet when no one else would. She was intent on doing something that proved Jesus was something more. Mary poured a jar of very expensive perfume over Jesus' feet. Then she wiped His feet with her hair.

The religious leaders wouldn't have approved of Mary's gift. Judas certainly didn't think it was wise. But Mary's gift left an impression on Jesus. Mary had moved to a place where she was certain that no one else was worth following. That's a perfect place to be.

Pray:

I will worship something, and if it's not You it's called idolatry. Help me do what Mary did. I want to make a big deal out of You. No one has given me more than You have or cared for me the way You do. No one can do what You do, and no one has a better plan than You. No one. Help me choose worship. Help me choose to worship You.

THE PEOPLE MISUNDERSTOOD

Read Exodus 19:1–19

Key Verse:

*On the morning of the third day, there was thunder
and lightning with a thick cloud on the mountain.
There was a very loud blast from a trumpet,
and all the people in the camp trembled.*
EXODUS 19:16 NCV

Understand:

- *Why might you be frightened if God showed
  the full extent of His power?*

- *How can God's laws show His character?*

Apply:

God is holy and He has never sinned. He's good. He
can't lie. He lives by the rules He gave to you. He
never says, "Do what I say, not what I do." He always
does what He says. He never makes a promise and
forgets to keep it.

This is the God Moses was going to meet at the
top of Mount Sinai. Moses realized there was great
responsibility in meeting with God. He could still

remember speaking to Him in the burning bush. The people had not spoken to God this way. This was their uncertain time.

The mountain displayed a violent light show, and the sound of thunder frightened the people. They watched Moses walk up the mountain and into the lightning, and soon they would get to know who God was by the rules He gave Moses. Having God's rules should have treated the symptoms of uncertainty, but the people misunderstood.

Pray:

If I size myself up with You, I lose every single time. You are bigger, wiser, stronger, and kinder than I have ever been or ever will be. You can do what I can't, and yet somehow You want to be my friend. You can arrive in a storm or show up in my quietest moments. You meet me the way I need to be met. I am grateful.

GOD'S OBITUARY

Read Matthew 27:45-56

Key Verse:

At once the curtain in the temple was torn in two from top to bottom. The earth shook, and rocks split apart.
MATTHEW 27:51 CEV

Understand:

- *Why did God demonstrate His power in such a profound way when Jesus died?*

- *How could people be confused about the events of the day?*

Apply:

When you read that Jesus died on the cross, you probably think about things like injustice or redemption. There was cruelty in Jesus' crucifixion and kindness in His act of love. There was jealousy on the part of powerful people, and there was a payment for sin.

God displayed power on Mount Sinai when Moses met with Him. It showed up in lightning and thunder. God displayed power on a killing hill called Golgotha in darkness and an earthquake. The people of Israel witnessed a spectacle. So did the people of

Jerusalem. The temple veil was torn in two, and people were no longer separated from God.

Certain leaders had conducted a public opinion campaign designed to ruin the credibility of God—and on the day of darkness and earthquake, they declared God dead even when they refused to believe that Jesus was God.

God didn't need an obituary. He was just getting started—and He was very much alive.

Pray:

You had a plan that most people couldn't believe. Your Son would come to live among us, and in order to rescue us, He would have to die defenseless and abandoned. Jesus' death brought rescue. Your power was on full display for all to see. These uncertain days were the start of a fully accessible relationship with You. Thanks for never needing an obituary, because I need You as much today as ever.

GOLDEN BOVINE
Read Exodus 32:1-14

Key Verse:

*He took what they handed him and made it into
an idol cast in the shape of a calf, fashioning it
with a tool. Then they said, "These are your gods,
Israel, who brought you up out of Egypt."*
Exodus 32:4 NIV

Understand:

- *Why would Aaron help the people become
even more uncertain?*

- *Have you ever considered a substitute for
God? What did you learn?*

Apply:

The Israelites were introduced to Egyptian gods
when they lived among people who worshipped
them. They saw the images of idols and saw that
people treated idols with honor. The Israelites even
might have come to believe that deities must be vis-
ible to be believed.

But it was an invisible God who led them out
of Egypt. That unseen God had been taking care
of their needs. Moses told them so. They wanted to

believe, but when Moses left the camp to talk to the one true God, the people started living in the past. They wanted a god they could see. In their uncertainty about the God their ancestors followed, they convinced Moses' brother Aaron to take their gold and make a god. They wanted something that could represent God, so Aaron made them a calf. They called this golden bovine the Lord. They made the wrong choice, and God was not pleased.

Pray:

When I'm confused about the truth, I can be convinced to believe a lie, live a lie, and tell lies to other people. I can try new options, explore different opinions, and end up believing I know nothing—or everything—I just can't be sure. The reason You exemplify a sure thing is that You don't change Your mind with every new opinion. Because You are certain, I can be too.

BUYING GOD

Read Acts 8:4-24

Key Verse:

When Simon saw that the Spirit was given when the apostles laid their hands on people, he offered them money to buy this power.
ACTS 8:18 NLT

Understand:

- *What makes you think that Simon didn't know God very well?*

- *When have you tried to make God something different than what He said He is?*

Apply:

The Simon in today's passage was not the disciple Simon (Peter). He was called a sorcerer or magician. He loved to impress people by doing things most people can't. His abilities made him appear powerful and important. He watched the disciple Philip talk about God's Spirit. All he could think about was having that kind of power.

The Bible says Simon believed and was even baptized, but he didn't fully understand. Simon believed in the *God product* and wanted to buy as much as he could. But God isn't a product. He's a gift. You can accept the gift, but you can't buy His power, love, or forgiveness.

God has never needed your money as if you were paying off a debt. He accepts your gifts as an act of worship.

Like the Israelites, Simon was trying to make God into something He wasn't. Simon wanted to worship God in the way that made sense to him. But Simon really needed to know God first.

Pray:

You can't be bought, sold, or bartered for, Lord. Your love is a gift and I'm meant to accept it, not run to a bank and take out a personal loan for it. I'm foolish if I think that You mean to make me important, famous, and impressive. Your plan for me is that I would grow to be more like You. I can do that when I stay close to You.

THE SNAKE
Read Numbers 21:4-9

Key Verse:

Then the LORD said to Moses, "Make a fiery serpent, and set it on a pole; and it shall be that everyone who is bitten, when he looks at it, shall live."
NUMBERS 21:8 NKJV

Understand:

- *What has ever made you wonder if God is in control?*

- *Why is it important to remember that God has always been in control?*

Apply:

God asked Moses to lead, and the people followed him into the wilderness where they wandered for four decades. You could say they were running out of patience, questioning his leadership, and wondering if God was real. They suffered from a short memory.

The people started a national protest. Moses and God were their targets. When they stopped following God, they broke His law. Snakes poured into the camp and started biting the sinning assembly. Then

God gave the people a simple way out of their predicament. Moses fashioned a replica of the snakes made of bronze. All they had to do was look at the bronze snake and they would be healed.

Imagine the uncertainty the people felt. They thought they were right to complain, but they ended up paying a price for rejecting the leadership God had prepared for them. The uncertainty continued after they started being bitten by the snakes. They needed a cure and no one had one—except God. In the midst of a death penalty, He brought rescue. He showed grace.

Pray:

Lord, I've been guilty of thinking You don't seem to have everything under control. I might even wonder when You're going to show up. I have been wrong to question. I have been hurt by not believing. Yet Your grace welcomes me to a better conclusion. You heal. You forgive. You show mercy when I least deserve it.

THE SAVIOR

Read John 3:14-21

Key Verse:

"As Moses lifted up the serpent in the wilderness, even so must the Son of Man be lifted up; so that whoever believes will in Him have eternal life."

JOHN 3:14–15 NASB

Understand:

- *What happens when you believe in Jesus?*
- *How can trusting in Jesus change things for you?*

Apply:

God painted Old Testament pictures of New Testament events—or maybe it's the other way around. The Israelites trusted something lifted up in the wilderness in order to be rescued and forgiven. Jesus would be lifted up on a cross in order for you to be rescued and forgiven. The healing He brings isn't relief from a snake bite. It's an answer to your sin problem.

Everyone has a sin problem, but not everyone focuses on Jesus for rescue. They shift their eyes away from the Rescuer and try to do better, work harder, and give more. They may never say it, but rescue seems like something someone else needs.

But sin is a poison that's killing you. It doesn't go away just because you don't take a day off or because you volunteer time at a shelter. You need someone to remove the poison so you can really live. Jesus does that, and when He rescued you, He brought life—a rich, meaningful, forever life.

Pray:

Father God, Jesus didn't die to impress me or even to make me feel bad. He was the only way I could be healed. There was no alternative or choice. It wasn't Jesus or three years of volunteer service. It wasn't Jesus or a lifetime of being nice to a neighbor. It was Jesus and nothing else. It was Jesus and nothing less. Help me keep my attention focused on Him today—and every day of my life.

THE NON-MESSENGERS
Read Deuteronomy 13:1-4

Key Verse:

*The LORD your God is testing you, to find out
if you love him with your whole being.*
DEUTERONOMY 13:3 NCV

Understand:

- *How would you describe a false prophet?*

- *How does knowing that God tests you
  change your perspective on things?*

Apply:

Tests can seem unexpected, unfair, and unkind. Some
people are horrible test takers. The anxiety builds
and memory takes a vacation. But God wants you to
think. He expects you to take His pass/fail test. He
doesn't grade on a curve or give extra credit. One of
His tests for the wandering Israelites was whether
they could identify false prophets. *Pass. Fail.* False
prophets were people who made a *good* case instead
of a *God* case. They sounded sincere, but they didn't
represent God very well.

False prophets shared enough truth that some

believed, and by the time these non-prophets began telling bold lies, they already had the masses believing they represented truth. So the people listened— and they failed the test.

Those who pass the test stand up against the false; they champion the truth; they call attention to the lies.

False prophets will always try to make God seem less important than He is and always has been.

Pray:

I'm engaged in Bible study. That means I'm studying Your Word—a lamp, an instruction manual. If Your Word doesn't say the same things I'm hearing, then give me hearing aids. Help me recognize truth by its reflection in the Bible. Help me recognize lies as something intentional or mistaken. But even if a lie is a mistake, never let me accept it as truth. And if something is truth, never let me dismiss it as if it's a lie.

PERSONAL RESEARCH

Read Matthew 7:7-20

Key Verse:

Watch out for false prophets! They dress up like sheep, but inside they are wolves who have come to attack you.
MATTHEW 7:15 CEV

Understand:

- *Why does Matthew describe false prophets as wolves dressed like sheep?*

- *Should you be concerned about false prophets? Why or why not?*

Apply:

If they were a GPS, they'd send you to the wrong location—*every time*. The good fruit they talk about seems to smell rotten. They say one thing but do something very different. It's true, the New Testament saw its fair share of false prophets, just like the Old Testament. They looked the part of a believer, but they had a bad habit of asking new questions that introduced old lies.

The Bible is clear—*avoid them*. Conduct personal research. If you want to know if what they say is what God has said, *explore the Bible*. Ask, seek, and knock on as many biblical doors as needed to learn God's truth. Don't let this be an uncertain time. There is no extra knowledge, new revelation, or creative interpretation that makes God's Word false. You can't remove a verse or passage from the Bible that contradicts a false prophet just because you like what they say. False prophets can be anywhere. They can say almost anything. And they don't like to be challenged.

Pray:

Help me attend Your university, Lord God.
What You teach never leads me anywhere but closer to You.
What others say needs to be brought to You for clarity.
I can read an emotional quote, see a beautiful sign,
or hear a likable personality. But when they say things
You haven't said, I need to stop listening to them
and start reading Your Word. Help me
believe the truth and reject all lies.

INDECISIVE
Read Judges 4:4–10

Key Verse:

Barak said to her, "If you go with me, I will go;
but if you don't go with me, I won't go."
Judges 4:8 NIV

Understand:

- *What is the difference between trusting God and relying on friends?*

- *Why is it dangerous to follow someone other than God?*

Apply:

To be uncertain means to be indecisive. People who are uncertain have trouble making decisions. There's an easy-to-understand reason that this is true. When you're uncertain, the only certain thing you can do is believe you can't make a decision.

When you were a child, you could hold someone's hand when you were scared, but once you've grown up, certainty means you trust God's directions.

Barak was supposed to be a soldier. He prepared

to win battles. But when he was called from the sidelines with ten thousand soldiers to help, he felt like he couldn't go alone. He wanted someone to hold his hand. He failed to trust God because he was frightened.

This Bible story isn't a condemnation of having good friends who stand with you. Everyone needs those. The problem comes when you know that you need God and His promises but then you also need something else.

For Barak this was evidence of uncertainty and unbelief. He seemed to be saying to anyone listening, "God is not enough."

Pray:

Lord, with You I can do things that will surprise and amaze me. With You I can do what You say I can do. There are times when I think I need more than You. While You've created me for relationships, You've asked me to follow You and do what You say. No hesitation. No reservation. Help me do that.

WHY COULDN'T I DO THAT?

Read Mark 9:14–24

Key Verse:

*"I asked your disciples to cast out the evil
spirit, but they couldn't do it."*
Mark 9:18 nlt

Understand:

- *Why should you expect the inability to follow
God's directions?*

- *Why shouldn't you settle for a lack of
personal faith?*

Apply:

The disciples had been following Jesus for many
months. Unlike Barak, they thought they were ready
to do what Jesus did. They had been successful in
some things, but this wasn't their day. They encountered a man who needed help. They were willing.
They just weren't able.

They really wanted to help. They wanted to
perform miracles. But they would need to wait for
more instructions. There was no shame in needing
to know more. There was no anger when they asked

for help. Maybe the big difference was that God gave instructions and promised victory to Barak, but that wasn't enough to move him to action. The disciples tried to do what only Jesus had done, and they ended up realizing they needed help—and Jesus offered it.

Learning from God and His Son instills courage in uncertain times. It offers answers when you have questions. It gives you the strength to obey. Be faithful in doing the things God says you can do. Then? Do more.

Pray:

Father God, help me learn how to do the things You need done. Help me recognize the needs around me. Never let me assume I should just know. Teach me. When I have learned and when You know I'm ready, then help me find the courage to do what would normally leave me uncertain. Help me honor You with my actions and follow You with my life.

BRING PURAH

Read Judges 7:1-22

Key Verse:

[The Lord said to Gideon,] "But if you are afraid to go down, go down to the camp with Purah your servant."
JUDGES 7:10 NKJV

Understand:

- *How is it helpful to have a friend stand with you when you are uncertain?*

- *How has God been able to move you from point A to point B in His plan?*

Apply:

Gideon didn't think he was very important. When God asked him to do something, Gideon replied with something that sounded like, "Are You sure? Ask the neighbors—they can vouch for the fact that I'm not important."

You might wonder what he had to worry about. God gave Gideon a victory, and He commissioned only three hundred men to help—even when thousands showed up.

Gideon was insecure, but perhaps his insecurity

was never more obvious than when God clarified all of Gideon's concerns and when it was time to go and see if what God promised was true. God told him he could take his servant, Purah, if he was afraid. *Gideon took Purah.* That bit of the story is easy to overlook. In uncertain times we don't always look at God's faithfulness first. There is usually a trip to the land of What-Ifs. That trip causes many people to doubt that God cares enough to help.

You may have never paid attention to Purah before today, but God used him to help Gideon trust and obey.

Pray:

Trusting Your decisions and accepting Your help are two things that take time and patience to master. Those who haven't known You long can find it unnatural to walk with You. Those who have done most things on their own can find it hard to accept help. I can be insecure, yet You've always loved me enough to offer Your help.

LIFE AFTER UNCERTAINTY QUICKSAND

Read Acts 9:26-31

Key Verse:

Barnabas took hold of him and brought him to the apostles and described to them how he had seen the Lord on the road, and that He had talked to him, and how at Damascus he had spoken out boldly in the name of Jesus.

ACTS 9:27 NASB

Understand:

- *How can your past make it hard for people to feel certain about your future?*

- *Why is it difficult to rebuild a good reputation?*

Apply:

Saul persecuted Christians. Under his watch, arrests were made. But once he met Jesus, everything changed. Try telling that to the Christians. They were chin deep in a pit of uncertainty quicksand. Could they trust a former enforcer of bad religious policy? Most knew people whom Paul had hurt.

Did a religious prison guard have the right to

talk about freedom in Christ? It was easier to reject his claims than to trust a man who'd never demonstrated kindness to those who followed Christ.

That was before Jesus brought Barnabas into Saul's life. When Barnabas made introductions, it had an impact. Uncertain people were still uncertain, but God was at work rehabilitating a bad reputation.

Saul, now Paul, was learning profound truth. *No one thought that was possible.* Barnabas helped Paul find places to share what he was learning. Those opportunities changed his life and the uncertainty of people who thought he couldn't be trusted.

Pray:

Lord, You tell me that my reputation is important, but because I fail, I'm glad to know You have plans that include reputation restoration. It can take time, but You never leave me and You bring people into my life who can help me. I will need You to make them known to me. I will need to accept the help You send.

UNCERTAINTY REVISITED

Read Ruth 1:1–18

Key Verse:

Long ago when the judges ruled Israel, there was a shortage of food in the land. So a man named Elimelech left the town of Bethlehem in Judah to live in the country of Moab with his wife and his two sons.

RUTH 1:1–2 NCV

Understand:

- *If Naomi told you her story today, would it be hard to hear her speak? Why or why not?*

- *Why do you think it was a help to Naomi when Ruth wanted to go with her?*

Apply:

When studying the book of Ruth, people often focus on what happened when Ruth and her mother-in-law, Naomi, returned to Bethlehem. Because this book is all about uncertain times, it might be important to know why Naomi left Bethlehem in the first place. Naomi's husband, Elimelech, took his family to Moab because there wasn't enough food in Bethlehem. Their sons got married in Moab and all seemed well until Naomi's husband and sons died.

Uncertain times had followed Naomi to Moab, and now she was alone. Or was she?

Her daughter-in-law Ruth insisted on following Naomi back to Bethlehem where uncertainty revisited. The family home had been empty and unrepaired for years. Food was still scarce for two widows with no income. Is it possible that God can use your moments of uncertainty to move you to a place of trust?

Pray:

Father God, when my plans fail and I'm feeling uncertain, please help me. When my reputation is in decline, restore me. When I need someone to help me, show me who will be helpful. I don't have answers, but I'll ask questions. There are things I don't possess, but I have hope. There is a future for me that is certain. Please lead me there.

CALL IT ANGST

Read Matthew 6:25-34

Key Verse:

*"Can any one of you by worrying
add a single hour to your life?"*
MATTHEW 6:27 NIV

Understand:

- *What are you most concerned about today?
  Will you talk to God about it?*

- *How often should you give your worries to
  God? Why?*

Apply:

Call it angst, misgivings, anxiety, fear, worry, or concern, but uncertainty has been everyone's roommate. It might be taking up space in your home right now. Jesus understood that worry is humanity's go-to response in uncertain times. He described worry using a variety of examples: birds, clothes, tomorrow.

In every case, God takes care of worry. He even makes it clear that if you spent every moment worrying, it wouldn't accomplish anything productive. Your worry will never change the outcome of anything. It won't make you live longer. It has no ability to calm your fear.

Worry distracts you from real answers. It consumes as much of you as it needs to cause you to stop thinking about God. It removes your ability to think rationally. It can even destroy relationships. But Jesus had an answer. He said there is no real reason to worry and you should focus on Him and then watch Him take care of your life.

Pray:

I have faced more uncertainty than I'd like, Lord. I'm afraid of more than I care to admit. I read the news, and I'm very concerned. But You're certain of the future, fear nothing, and know everything. You have no need to worry or be concerned about the outcome of anything. You can teach me to be certain that things will work out because You have already worked all things out.

KINSMAN REDEEMER

Read Ruth 4:1-12

Key Verse:

Then Boaz said to the elders and to the crowd standing around, "You are witnesses that today I have bought from Naomi all the property of Elimelech, Kilion, and Mahlon."
RUTH 4:9 NLT

Understand:

- *What stands out most to you about the way Naomi and Ruth were redeemed?*

- *Why did this redemption process change uncertain times for these two women?*

Apply:

The uncertainty of a foreign widow was a reality, but one man had the ability to remove that uncertainty for Ruth the Moabite. Enter Boaz.

He had noticed her when she arrived in Bethlehem. She had been allowed to wander in his fields and gather any leftover grain to eat. Another man was offered the opportunity to help, but he refused when he was made aware of the commitment involved.

Boaz became what is known as a *kinsman*

redeemer. It was just what Ruth and Naomi needed. He was someone who was part of the family and was willing to take full responsibility for family members and everything they owned. Boaz would marry Ruth and take care of her and Naomi for the rest of their lives.

With Boaz's single act of sacrificial kindness, the worry these two women felt was lifted. Boaz had committed to take care of them, and that commitment delivered confidence to the well-used door of uncertainty.

Pray:

I can only imagine how grateful Ruth must have been.
Her future was redeemed by someone she hardly knew.
An empty life became full in the act of redemption.
She could face each new day knowing she was not alone.
Worry seemed less important. This is redemption,
and it's what You have offered me.

CONNECTIONS TO A BETTER LIFE

Read Romans 3:21-31

Key Verse:

Now the righteousness of God apart from the law is revealed, being witnessed by the Law and the Prophets, even the righteousness of God, through faith in Jesus Christ, to all and on all who believe. For there is no difference.
ROMANS 3:21–22 NKJV

Understand:

- *Why is it good to remember you can't meet God's standard of perfection on your own?*

- *How can redemption remove anxiety?*

Apply:

You once lived in the refugee camp of uncertainty. It was a makeshift living space for the down-and-out, the misfits, and the anxious. No one wanted to live there, but no one had connections to a better life. All had sinned, and full acceptance required living up to God's standards. It was easy to give up in these disheartening conditions.

Residents couldn't care for each other because they were all trying (and failing) to take care of themselves. With each passing day, despair expanded like a balloon. This was before redemption. Then? You were invited to leave as one restored and redeemed.

God offered to take responsibility for you. He would take your worry and anxiety and in return give you a new life as part of His family. He promises to take care of you forever. Why would you want to go back to living like you did in the proverbial tent of uncertainty's camp? Why would you want others to stay there?

Pray:

You have given me the opportunity of forgiveness, Lord. I have access to Your love, grace, and family. I am never without the ability to talk to You or to read Your words. When I really understand that I can't do anything to make You decide to redeem me, I see more clearly just how incredible this gift really is.

ATTENTION, PLEASE

Read 1 Samuel 1:1-20

Key Verse:

[Hannah] made a vow and said, "O LORD of hosts, if You will indeed look on the affliction of Your maidservant and remember me, and not forget Your maidservant, but will give Your maidservant a son, then I will give him to the LORD all the days of his life."

1 SAMUEL 1:11 NASB

Understand:

- *Why would it have been easy for Hannah to give up her dream?*

- *How can God use your uncertainty to get your attention?*

Apply:

Hannah dreamed about having a child. One family member made fun of her, and her husband wondered why he didn't seem to be enough for her. The local priest accused her of being drunk when she asked God for a child. This was Hannah's recipe for personal uncertainty.

Everyone dreams about something they want to have or do. God doesn't always have the same dream, but when your purpose is aligned with His plan, then the following verse will make sense: "Delight yourself in the LORD; and He will give you the desires of your heart" (Psalm 37:4 NASB).

Uncertain times encourage you to observe God's next great story. Uncertain times can't be avoided entirely, but they can make you more aware of God's kindness.

While others laughed, were offended, or misunderstood, God made a way for Hannah and her son, Samuel.

Pray:

There will always be people who tell me I can't do something or will never be able to learn enough. They won't accept my dreams as worthwhile, and I might be their laughingstock. But You listen to my dreams and ask me to read Your response in the Bible. You tell me I can do what pleases You with Your help.

DON'T CRY
Read Luke 7:11-17

Key Verse:

When [Jesus] came near the town gate, he saw a funeral. A mother, who was a widow, had lost her only son. A large crowd from the town was with the mother while her son was being carried out.
LUKE 7:12 NCV

Understand:

- *Why would it be easy to assume the mother would be astonished?*

- *Describe the most memorable experience when God surprised you with an answer bigger than your prayer.*

Apply:

Her name is never given, but one woman lost her husband and was at the start of a funeral procession for her only son. Unlike Hannah, she wasn't waiting on new life—she was mourning for lives lost to time and circumstance. Jesus addressed her uncertainty in two words: "Don't cry" (Luke 7:13 NCV). The loss meant something to her. *Jesus noticed.*

She thought this day would be one she would

look back on as the threshold of profound grief. Yet Jesus had another plan that answered a longing she didn't know she could have. He touched the coffin and asked the dead son to get up.

This might have seemed like an insensitive response until the young man actually sat up. No one expected this. No one could answer dreams this way. No one but God.

This uncertain moment led to astonishment and praise among the people. God was honored, and a mother and son had an amazing story to share.

Pray:

Father God, You surprise uncertain people. You can give gifts no one expects. Any storm I go through just might become the story that invites others to bring their uncertainty to You. Walk with me in every moment so I can be sure that even when I'm confused, I'm not lost.

HELP WANTED

Read 1 Samuel 7:1-6

Key Verse:

The Israelites met together at Mizpah with Samuel as their leader. They drew water from the well and poured it out as an offering to the LORD. On that same day they went without eating to show their sorrow, and they confessed they had been unfaithful to the LORD.
1 SAMUEL 7:6 CEV

Understand:

- *Why would God make the people wait for the return of the ark of the covenant?*

- *How did it help to have Samuel remind the people of what was important?*

Apply:

The ark of the covenant was a sacred object God had told Moses to make. It followed the tabernacle everywhere it went until the Philistines engaged in battle with Israel and took it. The opposition forces soon discovered God wasn't happy about that. They tried to send it back, but that didn't work either. So the ark sat and the Israelites waited.

This was an uncertain time. The mood of the

people was described as "very sad" and they "begged the LORD for help" (1 Samuel 7:2 CEV). This situation wasn't resolved in a week or two. The Ark had been gone twenty years when Samuel stepped up. The people had been unfaithful to God, which led to their uncertainty. They said they wanted God's ark back, yet they still worshipped idols. They liked the sacred object but not the Sacred. They liked the things of God but not the God who made all things. That needed to change.

Pray:

Have I been guilty of loving the manger and cross while neglecting You? Have I enjoyed the stories and paid no attention to Your role in the lives of the people I hear about? I want to remember that my worst confusion is no match for You—the God who never changes.

INFERIOR DECISION-MAKING

Read Matthew 23:1-12

Key Verse:

[Jesus said,] "The teachers of the law and the Pharisees sit in Moses' seat. So you must be careful to do everything they tell you. But do not do what they do, for they do not practice what they preach."
MATTHEW 23:2–3 NIV

Understand:

- *How can just saying the right thing offend God?*

- *When is the right time to do the right thing?*

Apply:

Jesus recognized the Pharisees as being hypocrites. He'd seen their kind before. They said one thing and did something else. They wanted people to recognize them as superior but then made inferior decisions. They found people who made them feel better about themselves while insisting others didn't deserve to feel good about themselves. They had two faces and tried to hide one of them from the public. But Jesus saw, and He didn't like it.

When Jesus talked to His disciples, He wanted them to know that He had no use for people who acted that way. He expected more from His disciples. He wanted people to understand there is a closeness with God that is infinitely more valuable than pretending.

You will never be certain of anything when you can't remember the truth about who you are.

Pray:

When I want to impress others more than please You, then I'm setting aside relationship for applause. You say that if that's what I want, then applause is all I will get. Maybe that's why Jesus opposed the attitude of the Pharisees. They sought the applause of others yet lived out of sync with You. I want to please You. Sometimes that will mean I need to ask for forgiveness and admit I'm wrong instead of trying to convince others that I'm sinless.

DAVID'S CERTAINTY
Read 1 Samuel 17:32-49

Key Verse:

[David said,] "Everyone assembled here will know that the LORD rescues his people, but not with sword and spear. This is the LORD's battle, and he will give you to us!"
1 SAMUEL 17:47 NLT

Understand:

- *Why was David's certainty more than his ability to rescue sheep?*

- *If there are no limits to God's ability to bring certainty to your situation, then why is it so easy to be uncertain?*

Apply:

This story is a contrast between fear and faith, anxiety and trust, certainty and uncertainty. David entered the king's camp as a young man. He was too young to be a soldier but old enough to defend his family's sheep from savage predatory animals. When he arrived at camp, he witnessed a bit of pageantry. A giant was presented across the valley as a champion. He made fun of Israel and God. The soldiers of Israel seemed paralyzed with fear. But David had no idea why his older brothers and the rest of the army seemed so afraid.

David faced the sword of a powerful giant with nothing but a slingshot and stones and a deep trust in God. His not-so-secret weapon was God. He bested the giant and won the war for his country. Certainty gets things done. Uncertainty isn't sure there's a good time to start.

Pray:

Certainty isn't something acquired with age, because David was a young man. Uncertainty can affect us all. My perspective is key to how I respond, and when my perspective doesn't include You, I am uncertain. Help me respond like David did. When I need to stand up, don't let me find a chair to provide comfort on the sidelines.

FULLY TRUSTING

Read 1 John 5:14-20

Key Verse:

*If we know that He hears us, whatever
we ask, we know that we have the
petitions that we have asked of Him.*
1 John 5:15 nkjv

Understand:

- *How can confidence in prayer affect your
  confidence in your walk with Jesus?*

- *How can truth make you more confident?*

Apply:

Have you ever prayed wondering if your prayer
hit the ceiling and fell unheard to the floor? Have
you felt that you were the only one who heard your
prayers? You might come to believe prayer isn't as
helpful as you thought.

It's possible to say some words directed to God
and either not mean them or believe that they're
like a letter that winds up in the dead letter office of
the postal service, unread and unanswered. If God
doesn't listen to and answer prayer, then life should

be worse than any dystopian movie.

But John is talking about a belief that is just as strong as the faith of David when he challenged Goliath. John and David fully trusted in God, and their lives reflected His courage. Because God is alive, these men showed what an abundant life looks like. This kind of life confronts uncertainty with the certainty that God can take care of those things that seem out of control.

Pray:

I don't want to fake it to make it. I don't want to act as if I believe when I secretly doubt. This was the problem You had with the Israelites and with the Pharisees. There are times when You could have a problem with me. I come to You with uncertainty and leave with no answers. Help me be brave enough to really believe that You have always been able to do more than I ask or even think is possible.

OFFENDED

Read 1 Samuel 25:2-25

Key Verse:

One of the young men told Abigail, Nabal's wife, saying, "Behold, David sent messengers from the wilderness to greet our master, and he scorned them. Yet the men were very good to us."

1 SAMUEL 25:14–15 NASB

Understand:

- *What is your response when someone offends you?*

- *Does their opinion change the truth about the issue? Does it matter? Why or why not?*

Apply:

David wasn't king yet. He roamed the countryside helping people he encountered. Nabal was one of those men. So when David's men were hungry, he sent them to Nabal for help. Nabal refused.

In that moment Nabal introduced uncertainty for David and for his own family. Nabal wasn't interested in kindness or compassion. He refused to act like a friend. He would not be hospitable. Nabal seemed to enjoy being rude, and his behavior created great uncertainty for people who wanted peace.

Uncertainty can be introduced by people you thought were friends, extended by people you trusted, and ended by a God who doesn't consider those who meddle in the affairs of mankind to be an impediment to His plan. Trust the God who sets things right.

Pray:

I'm interested in how You want me to respond, Lord. I don't want to respond in a way that dishonors You. I may never know why it's so easy to become uncertain because of the uncivil response of another, but I can be certain You never respond that way to me. You have a plan, and it brings good to me. What's more, You give me strength to forgive the offenses of the careless. When the next frustration comes up, I want to remember that You straighten what's crooked and can help me accept what only You can change.

BETRAYED

Read Luke 22:1-6, 47-53

Key Verse:

Judas went to the leading priests and some of the soldiers who guarded the Temple and talked to them about a way to hand Jesus over to them.

LUKE 22:4 NCV

Understand:

- *What kind of emotions do you face when you are betrayed?*

- *Why do you think God allows the pain of betrayal?*

Apply:

Judas followed Jesus at His invitation. He walked with Jesus from town to town. He took care of the money for the small group of disciples. He believed Jesus was the Messiah. But Judas wanted a Messiah of his own description. He wanted a political leader who would remove Israel from Roman rule.

Jesus kept talking about the need to die. Would the Messiah need to die if He was meant to rule? So Judas chose to give in to his uncertainty. He accepted payment to betray Jesus. And then? *He betrayed Jesus.*

This wasn't a stranger or a professional bounty hunter. This was a man who was with Jesus every day. He was a witness to miracles that astounded, words that inspired, and lives that were changed. Yet in the end he chose to betray God's Son. Even so, his actions were no stumbling block to God's plan to redeem you.

Pray:

Uncertain times can make me angry, causing me to want to take control of the uncontrollable. It's like trying to dominate the weather by driving into a hurricane. I may think I can manipulate circumstances or change someone's opinion about one who has hurt me, but truth has a way of finding a voice no matter how much I might try to silence it.

PRAISE REMEMBERS

Read 2 Samuel 7:18-29

Key Verse:

Lord All-Powerful, you are God. You have promised me some very good things, and you can be trusted to do what you promise.
2 Samuel 7:28 cev

Understand:

- *Why might it have been important for the people to hear their new king praise God?*

- *Why do you think God is pleased to hear you remember where your help comes from?*

Apply:

David survived being chased by Saul; he was snubbed by Nabal; and he was made king by God. He wasn't perfect, but he understood the high value of praise.

His praise of God described fresh certainty in uncertain times. David remembered that he didn't deserve God's kindness; he recalled that God kept His promises; he couldn't help noticing that God is powerful and rescues His people. The new king found he had courage to enter the presence of God and thank Him, praise Him, and honor Him.

God used David to show how certainty is strengthened by recalling God's goodness. Count your blessings and make it a regular habit. Speak praise and listen to your own words. Honor God and allow people to see that giving God honor is important. No fear required. Like David, you too can give praise to a good God right now.

Pray:

You are the God who gave me life, and You have given me a plan to make it rich and full. I'm not sure why You recognize me, but You have, and I have become Your child. You're compassionate and have made Yourself known when life was incredibly hard. You've been kind when I've been rude. You've been faithful when I've been wishy-washy. You rescue, and I needed rescue. You have been good, and Your goodness will always be my companion. In Your love I am certain.

THE PLACE WHERE
MARY LIVED

Read Luke 1:41–55

Key Verse:

*"His mercy extends to those who fear him,
from generation to generation."*
LUKE 1:50 NIV

Understand:

- *What value is there in this praise from Mary's heart?*

- *How can praise change the way you view life?*

Apply:

She was young, and even though nothing made sense, Mary believed that God's promise of a child was irrevocable. Nothing could change what He had said, and she honored God in the same way King David had honored Him when he became king.

Mary's praise poured forth as she looked forward to the miracle. Mary believed it was more important to be sure and humble than to be uncertain and proud. When you think you know it all, you live in uncertainty because you are always afraid someone will prove you wrong. When you're sure you don't know it all, *but God does*, then a willingness to learn comes naturally. This was the place Mary lived. She was willing to learn and she was sure God was her Teacher.

She remembered God's mercy and mighty deeds. She was overwhelmed by His goodness. Mary was at the beginning of her own adventure, and praising the God who authored her story was just what she needed to do.

Pray:

Help me create my own psalm—words that express what bubbles from deep inside when I think about how good You are. I'll struggle to follow You if I think You're anything less than a good God. I want my memories of You to lead me to a place where praise is an easy response to Your love and kindness. I want to remember I need You and I can be certain I can learn from You.

WHAT I THINK OTHERS DESERVE

Read 2 Samuel 9:1–13

Key Verse:

The king then asked him, "Is anyone still alive from Saul's family? If so, I want to show God's kindness to them."

2 SAMUEL 9:3 NLT

Understand:

- *Why is kindness so often an unexpected response?*

- *How does kindness change the way you think about others?*

Apply:

The headlines might have read, "King David Takes in Grandson of King Saul." That was big news because most kings weren't kind to anyone from the last administration unless perhaps the person was a family member. What was especially notable in this case is that the man whom David took care of was handicapped.

Think about the uncertain times of this young

man named Mephibosheth. His father and grand-father were dead; he had a young son to take care of; he couldn't walk well; and he had no real way to earn money to care for himself. Most people would be wearing a path in the forest of depression, yet David stepped in showing mercy, expressing love, and demonstrating kindness.

King Saul had acted like an enemy. Why would King David help his grandson? The answer is found in David's words, "I want to show God's kindness to them."

When David showed God's kindness, the brakes were applied to Mephibosheth's uncertainty.

Pray:

Kindness may not always be my first response, but it's the response You expect from me. Love may not be what I want to give, but it's what You gave to me. Mercy may be the opposite of what I think others deserve, yet I have experienced it firsthand. When I follow You and do what You've done for me, I become more certain of Your kindness, love, and mercy, and I can be used by You to help ease the uncertainty in others.

DECLARED CLEAN

Read Luke 17:11-19

Key Verse:

One of [the lepers], when he saw that he was
healed, returned, and with a loud voice glorified
God, and fell down on his face at [Jesus'] feet,
giving Him thanks. And he was a Samaritan.
LUKE 17:15–16 NKJV

Understand:

- *What makes kindness and mercy good*
  companions?

- *How does gratitude fit with answered*
  prayer?

Apply:

The headlines might have read, "God's Son Heals
Foreign Leper." That was big news because most
people weren't kind to anyone from Samaria. If
this sounds familiar, it's because this story bears
a strong resemblance to what King David did for
Mephibosheth.

Jesus relieved the uncertain times these diseased
men endured under the fearful gaze of *the clean*.
These men asked for help, but once they were helped,

they became forgetful. Nine of the men saw life open up for them. They didn't have to hide away from the regular people anymore. They could be declared clean and rediscover normal. But one of these men was different—an outcast among the outcasts. He may have felt the least deserving. Yet mercy visited and he came away clean. How could he leave without saying thanks? So while the others walked away restored, this man recognized a miracle and spent a little more time with the One who showed what mercy looks like.

Pray:

You didn't have to send Jesus to rescue an outcast among outcasts, yet You did. You didn't have to demonstrate Your love in such a deep and meaningful way, yet I'm forgiven because You did. I know I don't deserve the gifts You offer, yet You never withhold them from me. I don't have to hide away ashamed and alone. But I can say thanks. I can spend time with You.

SOMETIMES LOVE SAYS NO

Read 2 Samuel 11:1-5

Key Verse:

So David sent and inquired about the woman.
And one said, "Is this not Bathsheba, the daughter
of Eliam, the wife of Uriah the Hittite?"
2 SAMUEL 11:3 NASB

Understand:

- *When has a sin left you uncertain?*

- *Why does sin leave everyone around you*
  uncertain?

Apply:

This is a case study in the growth of uncertainty in the presence of sin. King David saw a beautiful woman, thought about her, knew that she was married, and then chose to commit adultery with her.

The woman's name was Bathsheba, and she betrayed her husband by joining the king in the pursuit of physical passion. One other name is mentioned that you never hear much about—Eliam. He was Bathsheba's dad. He must have had his own list of uncertainties when he found out what happened.

Sin cannot improve certainty. It adds layers of complexity and only heightens the tension of uncertainty. Yet God was still able to restore the king from this sinful state. To be clear, God never approved of David's behavior, but He was highly interested in the condition of his heart. One of the great things God restored for King David was his certainty in God's goodness—and a love the king could be sure of.

Pray:

You never said I could do what I want. You gave rules to follow that require love for others. This isn't a selfish love that demands that others do what I want but rather one that looks to do what's best for others even if they might agree to sin with me. Sometimes love says no. It may be the hardest no I have to say, but You can help me say it, mean it, and live it.

COMPOUND UNCERTAINTY

Read John 8:1-11

Key Verse:

[The religious leaders said to Jesus,] "The law of Moses commands that we stone to death every woman who does this. What do you say we should do?"
JOHN 8:5 NCV

Understand:

- *What do you think were the motives of the religious leaders?*

- *How did Jesus' response change the thinking of those involved?*

Apply:

You've heard of compound fractures, right? This is when a broken bone compounds the severity of an injury by breaking through the skin, causing additional injury and infection.

There was a woman caught in sexual sin. *Uncertainty.* She was humiliated publicly, and Jesus was asked to act as her judge. *Compound uncertainty.*

Jesus is God's Son, and He had every right to declare the death sentence.

The religious leaders didn't know how Jesus would respond. *Uncertainty.* His response asked them to self-evaluate. *Compound uncertainty.* Those leaders left convinced that everyone sins; maybe they were even embarrassed by the memory of their own sins.

As with David, the woman's sins weren't excused but forgiven. Jesus gave her an opportunity to be restored. He gave her a road map out of her current situation. It started with His refusal to condemn her like the religious leaders wanted to do. *Certainty.* Then Jesus gave her advice that brings life—"Don't sin anymore" (John 8:11 NCV). *Compound certainty.*

Pray:

Father God, take the uncertainty of sin and lead me to compound certainty. Let my actions reflect my understanding that Your advice is to stop sinning. My choice to offend You leads me to the off-ramp to Uncertainty. But You can get me back on track. Help me be certain enough to follow You when I'd rather run away and hide. You never act as if my sin means nothing—it meant that Jesus came and died for me. Now that's something.

NATHAN'S PARABLE
Read 2 Samuel 12:1-15

Key Verse:

*David was furious with the rich man and said to
Nathan, "I swear by the living LORD that
the man who did this deserves to die!"*
2 SAMUEL 12:5 CEV

Understand:

- *Why can it be hard to recognize your
  own sin?*

- *How can you become uncertain when you
  recognize you have offended God?*

Apply:

A parable is a moral lesson told as a story. A very
memorable parable was told by the prophet Nathan:
A rich man had many sheep, but he was never quite
happy. A poor man had one sheep that he treated as
a pet. He didn't have much, but he thought his life
was good. When the rich man had a guest drop by,
he had a lot of sheep to choose from for the evening
meal. But he chose to keep his sheep. He sent a servant to take the pet sheep from his poor neighbor.

King David heard the story and became very angry. He saw the rich man as the worst kind of human being. He took something precious that wasn't his just because he wanted to. That was wrong. David knew it. He asked Nathan to tell him who this man was, because this rich man deserved the death sentence.

Imagine the uncertainty the king felt when the prophet told David that he was the rich man in the story. He didn't steal a pet lamb, but he took something that was worth much more to another man.

Pray:

Sometimes it's easier to remember a story. Thanks for sharing them with me. Help me understand the certainty of contentment. May I be satisfied with Your gifts and patient with Your timing. Help me cherish what You give me and not take what other people have.

LITTLE LAMB LOST

Read Luke 15:3-7

Key Verse:

Then Jesus told them this parable: "Suppose one of you has a hundred sheep and loses one of them. Doesn't he leave the ninety-nine in the open country and go after the lost sheep until he finds it?"

Luke 15:3–4 niv

Understand:

- *What makes the lost lamb important in this story?*

- *Why do lost sheep need to be found?*

Apply:

Rescue missions are about saving someone from danger. When you read the news, you read about the rescued but less about the concerned family members waiting at home. This is the idea behind a story that told of a shepherd on the search for one lost sheep. When the sheep was found, the entire neighborhood gathered for a block party to cheer the successful rescue.

Jesus compared people to sheep. When He

rescues someone, the angels cheer. This rejoicing is for the lost being found—and not for the ones already safe. Maybe that's because each one of us has our own rescue story.

Rejoice because you're rescued. Rejoice when God rescues the uncertain. Jesus is called the Good Shepherd, and you can cheer when He brings a lost sheep to join His flock. They will get to witness the next joy-filled celebration.

Rescue isn't a competition. It's an invitation to a family reunion that has been accepted. You didn't lose God's attention; you gained a family member.

Pray:

You came to rescue uncertain people. When I was lost, You found me. When I was uncertain, You gave me faith. You celebrate certainty and ask me to join You in celebrating those moments when someone understands that You've rescued them. This is the moment when confusion gives way to clarity and confidence replaces uncertainty.

A GOOD UNCERTAINTY

Read 1 Kings 3:1-15

Key Verse:

*[Solomon said,] "Give me an understanding heart
so that I can govern your people well and know the
difference between right and wrong. For who by
himself is able to govern this great people of yours?"*

1 KINGS 3:9 NLT

Understand:

- *Why is wisdom a great tool when you're
  uncertain?*

- *Who is the source of all wisdom?*

Apply:

Young Solomon was being given the keys to the
kingdom. He was the new king and had access to
every treasure gathered over the years. He could
make laws and enforce them. He could demand
tax and expect payment. But power is an amazing
responsibility that can flood your being with the lat-
est issue of *Uncertain Times*.

When God showed up in a dream to ask Solomon what he wanted as a gift, the uncertainty the

king felt led to a request that seems unexpected. He asked for wisdom. That was it. No request for three more wishes. No asking for more time to think. Perhaps it was uncertainty that made the decision easier.

Uncertainty can be the right tool in the right circumstance that will allow you to move from thinking you know enough to figure things out to knowing you need the kind of help only God can provide. These will be your most productive uncertain times.

Pray:

When I know more, I can understand more. When I understand more, I can let uncertainty go. You lead—I'll follow. You give—I'll receive. You offer—I'll take You up on the offer. I want wisdom and I need it. I can never become wise on my own because You hold the keys to real truth and not just today's pet theory. Let me draw from wisdom's well and drink deeply.

THE JOY ACCOUNTANT

Read James 1:2–25

Key Verse:

If any of you lacks wisdom, let him ask of God, who gives to all liberally and without reproach, and it will be given to him.
JAMES 1:5 NKJV

Understand:

- *What proof can you find that would suggest wisdom comes only after faith?*

- *Why does God want to give wisdom to you?*

Apply:

Revisit the first seven verses of today's study. It's a multistep process to help you reach a place of certainty. It all starts with trials and how you respond to them. It doesn't sound like fun, but don't give up.

Here's a breakdown of how this works: Trials come and your best response is joy. Why? Because once you capture this progression, you know that an initial response of joy improves every response you can make from this moment forward. Trials test your faith and faith helps you learn patience. Patience leads you to wait for the right tool, and when it arrives it is able to accomplish all you need. And if none of this makes sense, ask for wisdom and don't make doubt a dinner guest. When you believe, *you won't lack direction*. When trust is an option, so is uncertainty. Be ready for God's gifts. Doubt proves you need to start over again. Follow the steps. Repeat as needed.

Pray:

How many times have I given up when trouble comes because uncertainty won't let me find joy in knowing You will help? How many times have I tried to skip Your steps and found myself confronting confusion without Your wisdom? I'm asking for Your help, and I don't want to doubt that You will help. May I count the joy I have felt in those moments when I was patient and saw You help when I might have been convinced help wasn't coming.

DREAD

Read 1 Kings 18:1-19

Key Verse:

Now as Obadiah was on the way, behold, Elijah met him, and he recognized him and fell on his face and said, "Is it you, Elijah my master?"
1 KINGS 18:7 NASB

Understand:

- *What can make you uncertain that you should trust someone else?*

- *Why can God be trusted when people can't?*

Apply:

Elijah was a prophet-in-hiding. He wasn't ready to be found, and people had been looking. So when Elijah showed up where Obadiah was and told him to tell King Ahab he would meet him, it's not hard to understand the dread that filled Obadiah. Other people said they knew where Elijah was, but they didn't or Elijah was gone by the time they showed up. Obadiah thought telling the king could mean his execution if Elijah changed his mind.

King Ahab considered Elijah a troublemaker,

and he blamed him for the troubles in his country. Elijah and Obadiah followed God, but the king did not. Dread comes when there is a lack of trust. Faith brings certainty to the unknown.

There were lessons to be learned, and no one would be left out. Obadiah, Elijah, and King Ahab had different lessons to learn, but each would face uncertain times before God did unexpected miracles in the lives of His people.

Pray:

When unexpected and uncertain times happen, help me remember that I won't be the only person learning from moments I don't understand yet. Call that confusion or uncertainty, but You bring clarity to a future that seems blurry. You always see what I can't. While I'm concerned, doubtful, and worried, You wonder why that energy couldn't be channeled into God-sized trust. Help me with that kind of trust.

GET TO KNOW
Read Matthew 3:1-17

Key Verse:

Many of the Pharisees and Sadducees came to the place where John was baptizing people. When John saw them, he said, "You are snakes! Who warned you to run away from God's coming punishment?"
MATTHEW 3:7 NCV

Understand:

- *What made John so certain in what he said to the crowd?*

- *How does John's life inspire certainty in you?*

Apply:

Some thought going to see John the Baptist would be a show, a spectacle, or a diversion from everyday life. Some accepted his teaching and found a renewed sense of being God followers. He preached in the wilderness looking like a madman. He ate insects and talked about someone much greater who was coming into the world.

The religious leaders of the day wanted to squash anything that challenged their authority—and the wilderness crowds were becoming noteworthy. John spoke in figurative language and spoke of a tree being cut down and removed. He was referring to the religious leaders, and he called them snakes. He spoke of a coming judgement. He definitely wasn't making friends of these men of influence. But while he was certain he spoke the truth, the uncertainty they felt made them nervous, confused, and angry. They were the leaders. They didn't expect trouble. But it came, and it would lead many listeners to a new closeness with a God they had never before taken the time to get to know.

Pray:

Truth is sometimes very hard to hear. Open my ears so I can hear Your truth. Open my eyes so I can read Your Word. Open my mouth so I can tell of Your greatness. Make me certain. Help me trust. Give me the words someone needs to hear to explore certainty for themselves.

TACTICAL FORGIVENESS

Read 2 Kings 6:8–23

Key Verse:

*[Elisha said,] "You didn't capture these troops
in battle, so you have no right to kill them.
Instead, give them something to eat and drink
and let them return to their leader."*
2 KINGS 6:22 CEV

Understand:

- *How could Elisha's direction to give the
  enemy a banquet and send them home lead
  to feelings of uncertainty?*

- *Who exactly would be uncertain in this
  scenario? Why?*

Apply:

It was a response to a war declaration. Syria's king
pursued the people of Israel, and God gave a plan
that would allow Israel to win the war. Sometimes
in war the opposition died in the fighting or were
taken prisoner, but that was not the case this time.

Elisha was asked what they should do with the
prisoners. His response must have confused a lot
of people. It likely left the prisoners uncertain. The

end result was a lavish meal and a free ticket home for all prisoners. It was an act of mercy that no one expected. Some thought it was bad military policy.

Yes, this story included chariots of fire and help from God in ways that meant no opposition could win, but it also provided an ample taste of grace, mercy, and forgiveness when people were uncertain those things existed. God took something bad and made it good. There was no longer a reason to pursue an adversary that God had vanquished. This unexpected lesson still takes place in the lives of believers today.

Pray:

Help me embrace this example of forgiveness.
Help me believe that when You take care of something,
I'm no longer in any position to retaliate.
Help me learn that when I don't see others
as enemies, I can see them as friends.

STEP AWAY

Read Matthew 5:38-48

Key Verse:

[Jesus said,] "You have heard that it was said, 'Love your neighbor and hate your enemy.' But I tell you, love your enemies and pray for those who persecute you."
MATTHEW 5:43–44 NIV

Understand:

- *In what ways could your response to others change if you took this passage seriously?*

- *How could treating others with love allow you to view God's love with greater certainty?*

Apply:

The teachings of Jesus were intriguing because they were so different from what most expected. Things like love, don't hate. Bless, don't curse. Pray, don't gossip. Reach out, don't keep what you're learning to yourself.

Today's Bible study invites you to step away from the courtroom of justice to see the struggle diffused by mercy. It's easy to take a single view of love and think you're doing well. You love your family and friends, right? Is that enough? Not really. *Love your enemies too.* If you think that means you need to love *everyone*, then you've accepted the accurate view.

Maybe the most compelling reason Jesus spoke these words was that God has always exemplified this principle; He has always extended compassion to humans who fail to consider His love. They have done their best to hurt God, yet He never stops loving them. He continues to show mercy when justice seems an acceptable response.

Pray:

You're the Great Forgiver, the Creator of love, and the Author of mercy. I want to see others as perfect candidates for all that You've given me. Help me see others as needing all that You offer, because all that You offer is all they need. Give me a heart that expands with Your purpose and spills love into the lives of those who need to know that You make this impossibility possible.

THE REPORT IS BAD

Read 2 Kings 19:1-19

Key Verse:

[King Hezekiah prayed,] "Now, O Lord our God, rescue us from his power; then all the kingdoms of the earth will know that you alone, O Lord, are God."

2 Kings 19:19 NLT

Understand:

- *What is your first response when hearing something that fills you with dread?*

- *How can shifting your focus to God help reduce or even eliminate uncertainty?*

Apply:

You receive a report. It's bad news. Your company is downsizing and they have no room for you. They let you go. The doctor found something. He's not hopeful. Your spouse has had a change of heart. They now have a change of address. Bad news shows up and alters what felt like certainty.

King Hezekiah got one of these notices. The entire nation heard the report of one man who promised destruction was coming. He emphasized the idea that even God Himself could not help. A tsunami wave of uncertainty chased the people home.

Routines would be altered, jobs would change, and people might be forced to move or be killed for disobedience. This was the logical thought process in response to the bad news declaration. The saving grace in this storyline is that God wasn't the one declaring destruction. The king didn't enlist a larger army. He enlisted the help of God.

Pray:

If I pay attention to the news, I can become worried. So many bad things have happened, can happen, or might happen. But I can't control that. Only You can. The news I read or see is only part of the story. You get the final word. Help me trust You more than the headlines, believe You more than breaking news, share You more than the special bulletins.

LIVING THROUGH DELAY

Read John 11:1-44

Key Verse:

The sisters sent to Him, saying, "Lord, behold, he whom You love is sick." When Jesus heard that, He said, "This sickness is not unto death, but for the glory of God, that the Son of God may be glorified through it."
JOHN 11:3–4 NKJV

Understand:

- *Why is it easy to assume the worst and accept uncertainty as normal?*

- *Why should you rethink what's true in moments of uncertainty?*

Apply:

Imagine being asked to help someone you love in a matter of life and death. Do you take a vacation or stay in town for a business meeting? Most people would leave what they're doing so they can help where they're needed. *That's not what Jesus did.* He delayed His departure knowing His friend Lazarus would die before He arrived.

That left two uncertain sisters, Mary and Martha, and twelve uncertain disciples. What was Jesus doing? It seemed He didn't care. When Jesus arrived at the tomb, we read that He did something very human—*He wept.* Then Jesus commanded a man who had been dead for four days to come back to life and walk out of the tomb.

That wasn't the expected outcome of uncertainty, but, as with Hezekiah's predicament in the Old Testament, when God authors the outcome, all the uncertainty in the world can't change it.

Pray:

Unconventional might be a good way to describe the way You answer prayer, but Your answers are only unconventional to me. You answer very specifically and in a way that demonstrates Your power and love. Help me remember that Your blessings don't always seem to fit my definition of blessings. You can help, but I don't get to choose how You help.

EMPTY AND UNCERTAIN
Read 2 Kings 25:1-17

Key Verse:

*Nebuzaradan the captain of the guard,
a servant of the king of Babylon, came to
Jerusalem. He burned the house of the LORD, the
king's house, and all the houses of Jerusalem.*
2 KINGS 25:8–9 NASB

Understand:

- *Why is sadness a companion in uncertain times?*

- *Why might it be important to consider what God may be teaching you during these times?*

Apply:

The streets were empty and covered in debris. Smoke still rose from smoldering piles. Most of the people were gone. Some had been killed. Those who caused this destruction would be back. The situation was surreal. It was reality for the people who once greeted neighbors and bought produce in the market. This had been home, but no longer. It had been taken from them, and no one could rebuild alone. The circumstances felt hopeless.

Nebuzaradan was a hired gun. He enforced the edict from Babylon. He could not have succeeded if it weren't part of God's plan. If that sounds harsh, please remember that God can take uncertain times and use them to draw (or draw back) people to Himself.

When the people refused to listen, God sent prophet messengers to warn them that this would happen. They didn't want to believe, and they chose not to believe. No one wanted *this* promise to be true. Yet uncertain times arrived and would stay for seventy years.

Pray:

I love to read about mercy, grace, and forgiveness, but sometimes I forget that You want obedience over sacrifice. You want me to do the right thing rather than just feel compelled to admit I was wrong later. Some of my uncertain times have been due to my own choices. I live through the consequences while I reconnect to Your plan.

A TROUBLE OPPORTUNITY

Read John 16:4-15, 25-33

Key Verse:

[Jesus said,] "I told you these things so that you can have peace in me. In this world you will have trouble, but be brave! I have defeated the world."

JOHN 16:33 NCV

Understand:

- *How can trouble lead you to a place of peace?*

- *How can God use uncertainty to alter your life story?*

Apply:

You've read the word *uncertain* many times so far in this Bible study, and it makes sense—especially considering this book covers the uncertain times faced by humans like you. Call it confusion, red flags, a check in your spirit, or trouble, but uncertainty is common to every single human. The biggest difference is in how each person responds.

You can have peace when troubled days come. God promised trouble, and He also promised to be with you. He promised He would win. Don't sweat trouble as if it has the power to write your final chapter. It doesn't. *It never has.*

All kinds of voices will speak doom and gloom. Listen to God. He speaks the language of certainty, and He sent His Spirit to teach it to you. Trouble simply becomes the opportunity for God to step in and flip the script. He creates plot twists so that the ending is nothing you expected but everything you needed.

Pray:

I can have goals and plans and then stick to them with such a tight grip that it seems I don't want Your plan. My choices can make it seem like Your plan isn't welcome. I might even wonder why it seems like You're interfering in my life. Help me realize that trouble presents the opportunity to trust You to deliver a better outcome than my failed plans.

NEWS FROM HOME

Read Nehemiah 1:1–11

Key Verse:

When I heard this, I sat down and cried.
Then for several days, I mourned; I went without
eating to show my sorrow, and I prayed.
NEHEMIAH 1:4 CEV

Understand:

- *How can uncertainty show up in news from home?*

- *What event that happened to someone you care about caused uncertain times for you?*

Apply:

They say there's nothing better than news from home. Nehemiah learned that not all news is good; not all stories are happy.

Nehemiah worked in the palace of a foreign king. He was once a citizen of Israel, before the exile. Now he filled the cup for the king, and he'd earned the king's respect.

Word reached Nehemiah that the walls in Jerusalem were broken and the gates burned. These gates had signaled protection for the people, safety from the strongman, and caution to the con artist. Now? People could come and go, take what they wanted, and rejoice in the destruction of God's city. So Nehemiah sat, wept, and prayed. It was his declaration of uncertainty. He believed that the only true answers would come from God.

Certainty returned to Nehemiah when he celebrated God's faithfulness and remembered His promises. Nehemiah didn't know how things would turn out, but the news from home turned his heart in a better direction.

Pray:

My thoughts have limits. I think about the way things once were, and I feel sad about the way things have changed. People I know get sick. Places I've been change over time. When I visit, I can only lament that my memory no longer connects with reality. Help me learn from Nehemiah. Help me care about people enough to help them through the uncertainty of change.

RENEWED CERTAINTY

Read Luke 24:13-35

Key Verse:

They asked each other, "Were not our hearts burning within us while he talked with us on the road and opened the Scriptures to us?"

Luke 24:32 NIV

Understand:

- *Why can uncertainty come when you don't know the full story?*

- *What changed inside when you first realized how important Jesus really is?*

Apply:

Things had changed. The two had witnessed the miracles of Jesus, the words He spoke, and the kindness He shared. Now? They were told He was dead. The stranger could hear their sadness. They spoke of the good old days. The man knew what they were talking about. He'd lived those days. *He had more to share.*

These were uncertain times on the road to Emmaus. The future they hoped for seemed crushed. They thought everything would change because of

Jesus, but then there was a trial, a cross, and a tomb. Perhaps they were blinded by grief, but they didn't recognize the stranger. They had been speaking with Jesus, and He listened to them. He spent time with them. He helped them see the truth. He was alive. He fulfilled prophecy. He was the Messiah.

If heaven was home, then these two were waiting for news from home, and it was shared by the Maker of home and earth.

The answers they needed came from Jesus. Hope was restored, and certainty shouted that a better day was to come.

Pray:

Help me recognize the beauty of Your gifts, the wonder of Your salvation, and the value of being bought from the grip of sin. I want to recognize Your sacrifice and treat You with honor. Thanks for hearing my story when I feel lost and abandoned. Thanks for reminding me that I'm never really alone.

THE ADOPTED ORPHAN GIRL BECAME QUEEN

Read Esther 4:1–17

Key Verse:

Mordecai sent this reply to Esther: "Don't think for a moment that because you're in the palace you will escape when all other Jews are killed."
ESTHER 4:13 NLT

Understand:

- *What can make it easy to believe that trouble is something only other people face?*

- *Why is denial a problem when you are facing hard times?*

Apply:

Esther was an orphan. She was a foreigner now living in Susa with a cousin who adopted her. Against all odds, she would become queen. *That shouldn't have happened.* But this bizarre path was less about Esther and more about God's love for His people.

God knew things. He knew that a man named Haman would get the king to sign a bad law. He knew the king would sign it. He knew that this new law would allow people to kill anyone who was a Jew. Yet there was a new queen. The king loved her. *God loved her.* She could ask for help, but if the king didn't want to help, then he could kill Esther.

She asked her cousin to help her manage this uncertain time by praying for her. He enlisted others to join him. God helped an uncertain young woman living in uncertain times to trust Him for certain victory.

Pray:

I can face trouble when I know that You'll be walking with me through it and be waiting at the end of it. I don't have to know what You're doing to know that You're good. I don't have to have all the answers to know You're trustworthy. I don't have to feel safe to know that I am rescued by You. Worry could be my response. Help me choose faith instead.

A KING LIKE HIM

Read Matthew 2:1-15

Key Verse:

Behold, an angel of the Lord appeared to Joseph in a dream, saying, "Arise, take the young Child and His mother, flee to Egypt, and stay there until I bring you word; for Herod will seek the young Child to destroy Him."
MATTHEW 2:13 NKJV

Understand:

- *In what ways can you identify with the jealousy that resulted in Jesus' move to Egypt?*

- *How does thinking of this time in Jesus' life make you think that He understands you?*

Apply:

They were men. Wise men. These wisdom seekers sought and found Jesus. They brought and shared gifts. They left wiser for being in the presence of God's Son.

Before these men made it to Bethlehem, they stopped to talk to King Herod. They knew what he didn't. Jesus had been born into the world of humans, and there would never be another king like Him.

Like Esther, Jesus was sent for just the right time to save people from spiritual death. For a while He was sent to a foreign country to live. God rescued Him from a law that King Herod passed that would have meant His death. Jesus would die for you—but first He had many things He needed to do, show, and teach.

Jesus lived the life of a human. He understood unkindness, prejudice, and bullies. He lived with bad laws and poor leaders. He lived to love you, and His law for you is love.

Pray:

Father God, Your Son faced bullies and prejudice at such a young age. People can be cruel. You know that better than anyone. I want to praise You for understanding my hardest days. Help me realize that the pain Jesus endured is a reminder that You have always loved me.

ENVY BAD DECISIONS?

Read Psalm 73:1-23

Key Verse:

As for me, my feet came close to stumbling, my steps had almost slipped. For I was envious of the arrogant as I saw the prosperity of the wicked.
PSALM 73:2–3 NASB

Understand:

- *When have you faced uncertainty because people who made bad decisions ended up getting good things?*

- *Why should you feel compassion for people who don't think they need to follow Jesus?*

Apply:

Uncertain times can find you placing an order for instant delivery of envy. You think you're not in the place you'd like to be, but it seems other people always get what they want. You follow God. *They don't.* You do your best to love people. *They make fun of others.* Is life fair? It might not seem like it.

God promised you would have trouble, but did He give a free pass to those who don't love Him? Maybe the best reason Psalm 73 is in the Bible is because you have probably felt that way.

The psalmist came to a conclusion. He'd been shortsighted. He was only looking at the life he lived at that moment. There would come a time when he would be with God and those who refused to follow Him would not. The psalmist had access to the wisdom of God, while the non-followers could only guess. Who would need to envy that?

Pray:

I'm grateful that I will always have You. You don't run away when I find myself envying others who seem to have it easier than I do. When I don't feel like I have much, help me remember that I have You and You have me. Help this truth change the way I think about others who might only have something to look forward to in the next delivery truck.

FOOLISHLY JEALOUS
Read Titus 3:3-11

Key Verse:

In the past we also were foolish. We did not obey, we were wrong, and we were slaves to many things our bodies wanted and enjoyed. We spent our lives doing evil and being jealous. People hated us, and we hated each other.
TITUS 3:3 NCV

Understand:

- *Have you left foolishness in the past? Why would that be God's plan for you?*

- *What role should jealousy play in your life? Why?*

Apply:

Did you notice that the verse above says that foolishness existed in the past? Maybe the author realized that recalling past mistakes can give you a present reason to avoid them in the future. You remember what your life was like when you didn't obey God, when you made wrong choices, and when jealousy and hatred were second nature and a first response. You remember because you shouldn't forget those things that keep you from God.

Foolishness is a sense of uncertainty that forgets God's kindness, love, and mercy. He's the One who can rescue. You could never save yourself. He's the One who pours into your life. You can never be fulfilled on your own. He's the One who gives good words to speak. With His help you can stay out of foolish arguments.

There's no need to be envious of people who still live in that place of foolishness. It doesn't exist in the past for them, and it could influence *you* to embrace wrong thoughts and actions.

Pray:

I want to keep foolishness in the past, Lord. Make envy an unpleasant memory. I want my life to be marked by obedience and love. Help me express kindness and mercy. Show me the way to help others see You in me. Life with You isn't a competition; it's the opportunity to walk with others on the way to meet You.

DOWNTOWN UNCERTAINTY
Read Psalm 119:97-114

Key Verse:

I am in terrible pain! Save me, LORD,
as you said you would.
PSALM 119:107 CEV

Understand:

- *How can pain usher you into the presence of uncertainty?*

- *How can a friendship with God impact the pain you feel and the uncertainty you experience?*

Apply:

Pick your pain. It could be physical, mental, emotional. It might dwell in the past or in the present, or it might rob you of hope for the future. Pain comes to everyone. You hate it. *Everyone does.* But God is the answer to pain, because while pain is a temporary condition, He is forever.

Pain may have been the exact thing that convinced the psalmist to say, "Your word is a lamp that gives light wherever I walk" (Psalm 119:105 CEV). He knew who could help.

You want to see where you're going, right? *God's Word.* You want to know the obstacles you will face? *God's Word.* You want to know how to avoid spiritual speed bumps? *God's Word.*

There are a lot of ways you can put your pain on mute, but it will always come back full volume. God never intended for you to merely mask the pain but rather to face it, deal with it, and put it in the past. When you don't? Welcome to another round of uncertain times. God's lamp + God's light = certainty.

Pray:

Facing hurt seems like I'm earning a degree in advanced isolation, but that's not what You want. You don't ask me to run from You until I get better. You want me to come to You because I am sick—and You're the Great Healer. Your companionship will mean more to me than the runaway thoughts that always leave me in the middle of downtown Uncertainty.

LIVING WITH THORNS
Read 2 Corinthians 12:1-10

Key Verse:

Therefore, in order to keep me from becoming conceited, I was given a thorn in my flesh, a messenger of Satan, to torment me. Three times I pleaded with the Lord to take it away from me.
2 CORINTHIANS 12:7–8 NIV

Understand:

- *Why do you think God doesn't always remove difficulty from your life?*

- *How might pain transform your friendship with God?*

Apply:

You might call it chronic pain. Paul referred to it as a thorn in his flesh. This kind of pain is irritating. People might not even be aware of your hurt, but it never seems to leave. You've tried everything to relieve the pain.

Illness is a potent uncertainty. You don't know if you can take it another day. You just want the irritation to end. Paul wanted that too. When he couldn't stand it anymore, he asked God to take it away, but

He didn't. This wasn't because God didn't listen, and it wasn't because He didn't care. Sometimes God has a purpose behind the pain. God didn't send Paul's pain—He just didn't take it away.

Paul had his *thorn*, and while it may have seemed debilitating, God used Paul in a mighty way. His effectiveness wasn't dependent on whether he had an easy life or pain-free body. It could even be argued that the pain urged Paul to rely on God even more.

Pray:

If I got everything I wanted, it's easy to imagine I would have more money than I need, every shiny thing I was interested in, and perfect health. Your Word is filled with stories of people who were sick, those who died, and those who lived with pain—people like me. Help me embrace Your certainty in the midst of my pain.

GOD'S LOVE IS CERTAIN

Read Psalm 139:1-18

Key Verse:

*O Lord, you have examined my heart
and know everything about me.*
Psalm 139:1 nlt

Understand:

- *Why can you feel uncertain knowing that
  God is aware of everything about you?*

- *How can this uncertainty become assurance
  of God's love?*

Apply:

There's a children's Christmas song you've probably heard that mirrors the uncertainty many people feel about God. "He sees you when you're sleeping; he knows when you're awake. He knows if you've been bad or good, so be good for goodness' sake!" If it seems like a lot of surveillance from one jolly and rotund man, then you should know that a good God with great love knows literally everything about you. *Nothing* you do escapes His notice.

When you gossip, *He hears it.* When you're rude,

He sees it. When you hate, *He knows it.* But rather than feeling as though your personal space is being invaded, you should know that no matter what you've done, nothing can convince Him to stop loving you—His love is certain.

Life can seem uncertain if you feel as if God has had it with you. Certainty comes in knowing He loves you even when you've had it with yourself.

Pray:

When I try to convince myself that I've hidden something from You, I'm only fooling myself. Everything done in secret and all those things that are fully seen are added to the list of things You know about me. Thanks for loving me in spite of my failings, shame, and fear. Help me embrace the certainty of Your love. I'm certain I need it.

WEAK REBELS

Read Romans 5:1-11

Key Verse:

But God demonstrates His own love toward us,
in that while we were still sinners, Christ died for us.
Romans 5:8 nkjv

Understand:

- *Why can it be surprising to know that God loves rebels?*

- *When is the right time for rescue? Why?*

Apply:

You couldn't be counted on. You couldn't be trusted. God had a lawbook, and you said, "No, I won't follow it." That's what everyone looked like from God's perspective when Jesus died a criminal's death. Our actions said we wouldn't love God, but He said, "I've always loved you."

You might want to do everything yourself, but you don't have the strength. You know you can't do everything on your own, yet there have been times you used what little strength you had to tell God you didn't need His help. You'd think God would get tired of all the uncertainty. Maybe He just gets sad.

There's no secret in His rescue plan. It's simple. You need rescue from sin. *He rescues.* You can accept or reject His rescue, but that's the plan. You can fight against it, tell others it's ridiculous, make fun of those who've been rescued, and the end result is still·God offering you rescue.

Feeling uncertain without rescue makes sense. But feeling uncertain after you've been rescued should point you to a place of trust.

Pray:

I don't know anyone who would sacrifice his life for an enemy. But I know You, and that's exactly what You did. Humans fought against You then, and I do it now. Jesus cleared the path so I could find You, talk to You, and allow You to rescue me. Help me stop giving in to rebellious thinking. Help me accept Your love and discover new life.

CERTAINTY OF PRAISE

Read Daniel 3:1-30

Key Verse:

These three men, Shadrach, Meshach and Abed-nego, fell into the midst of the furnace of blazing fire still tied up.
DANIEL 3:23 NASB

Understand:

- *Why would it have been easy to do what the king commanded?*

- *Why was it important that these men follow God's command?*

Apply:

Three longtime friends were captives in Babylon. They knew God, loved Him, and always sought to take His side. They weren't rebellious toward the king they served in this foreign land, but they chose not to violate God's law—even when the king commanded them to do so.

When the king made a statue that everyone was to bow down to and worship, the friends knew no gray area was involved. They couldn't do it. Even when they were given a second chance, their answer was a clear, "No."

Would God rescue these three men from the king? The situation didn't look promising when the king grew angry. It didn't look promising when he sentenced them to incineration in a blazing furnace. It didn't look promising when they were in the middle of the flames.

But it was then that any uncertainty they may have felt became the certainty of praise. They walked in the flames and did not get burned. Their faithfulness resulted in a story of God's blessing that would be shared for generations to come.

Pray:

*If Your idea of blessings doesn't look like mine,
then I need to see blessings from Your point of view.
Sometimes a future blessing is wrapped in trouble and
heartache. Sometimes I'm faced with uncertainty so that
when You do something miraculous, only You will get
the credit and I will remember Your mercy even more.
Bring on the blessings and take the next step with me.*

OPPORTUNITY AT MIDNIGHT

Read Acts 16:16-40

Key Verse:

At midnight Paul and Silas were praying and singing hymns to God, and the prisoners were listening to them. Suddenly there was a great earthquake, so that the foundations of the prison were shaken; and immediately all the doors were opened and everyone's chains were loosed.
ACTS 16:25–26 NKJV

Understand:

- *If you were unjustly imprisoned, how easy would it be to sing praises to God? Why?*

- *What kind of impact would this concert have on the other prisoners?*

Apply:

If you've ever been accused of something you didn't do, then you probably understand a little of what life was like for Paul and Silas. Likely no one would blame you for seeking legal advice on how to gain your freedom. But Paul and Silas chose a different response. They engaged in a two-voice worship service in jail. They had a captive audience—literally—and they listened. These two had followed God, and their faithfulness caused an uproar among some who insisted on finding fault.

God used the unjust actions of others to allow prisoners to hear about a good God. And when He rescued the two from prison in an earthquake, God also orchestrated the rescue of the jailer who needed the hope Paul and Silas had. No experience is wasted in God's plan. The uncertainty of others means an opportunity for those who have the certainty of Jesus.

Pray:

I don't often consider the possibility that my stories of suffering can provide opportunities to help others see You. My certainty in You can press the pause button on uncertainty for others. You lead me through, and I want to let others know I'm grateful.

DEN DELIVERANCE

Read Daniel 6:1-23

Key Verse:

At daybreak the king got up and ran to the pit. He was anxious and shouted, "Daniel, you were faithful and served your God. Was he able to save you from the lions?"
DANIEL 6:19–20 CEV

Understand:

- *What does this passage teach about allegiances?*

- *What can you learn from this passage about how to respond to authority figures?*

Apply:

Uncertainty is always close by when you believe that you're doing the right thing but your actions are not well accepted by others. You figure that if you're doing the right thing, others should applaud your commitment to truth and right living.

This scenario can feel a bit like being caught between a rock and a hard place. If you do the right thing some will still find ways to accuse you. If you do the wrong thing, it will always be the wrong thing.

You may feel like you really have no option. Daniel proved, like others before and after him, that you can follow God and He will make a way through any injustice that might follow.

The king didn't want to throw Daniel in the lions' den, but he had made a rash decision and signed a law he regretted. When Daniel prayed to God, the human punishment was a night with lions. Daniel survived because God protected him. God was made famous through the obedience of a man who spent time talking to God inside and outside the den.

Pray:

Help me be certain that following You is the most important thing I can do. Help me deal with any uncertainty that challenges this choice. Lead me through the injustice that always fails to recognize You. Help me be strong for Your name's sake.

LOVE UNSTOPPABLE

Read Romans 8:28–39

Key Verse:

What, then, shall we say in response to these things?
If God is for us, who can be against us?
ROMANS 8:31 NIV

Understand:

- *Why was it important for Paul to list so*
  many things that can't change God's love
  for us?

- *Reread the key verse. How does it relieve*
  uncertainty?

Apply:

One of the biggest reasons you take note of uncertain days on the horizon is because you've forgotten the greatest thing you possess—*the love of God*. Nothing else you can lose is even a close second *if* this were a competition. *It's not.*

The beginning and end of life, spiritual power and influence, things that happen today or next year, and things that could impact you from any direction are all reasons you can assume it's sensible to be insecure and uncertain. As a result, you may strive to avoid chaos, conflict, and confusion at all costs. Safety might become a vital component of anything you choose to do.

But nothing—nothing—can change the most important thing God has offered you: *love*. Consider that when God loves you, you can be certain that neither your hardest day, nor your greatest trouble, nor the worst persecution, nor extreme hunger, nor homelessness, nor any dangerous situation, nor any weapon known to man has any influence over God's willingness to continue loving you. Uncertainty on the issue is no longer welcome.

Pray:

Your love is greater than my uncertainty.
Your grace exceeds my insecurity. Your mercy reduces
my apprehension. And at the end of my life I will
be in Your presence, having taken the opportunity
to believe that You have always loved me and
will never stop. Arrest the development of
uncertainty from this moment forward.

COME HOME
Read Hosea 1:2-11

Key Verse:

When the LORD first began speaking to Israel through Hosea, he said to him, "Go and marry a prostitute."
HOSEA 1:2 NLT

Understand:

- *What was the most surprising part of this passage? Why?*

- *How are you impacted by Hosea's faithfulness to his unfaithful wife?*

Apply:

Hosea's life was a living object lesson in trust. His faithfulness would have left most people uncertain. This prophet was to tell people to come back to God. Hosea experienced firsthand how it felt to live with the unfaithfulness of others and still love them.

God asked Hosea to marry a prostitute. He made it clear that this wife would be unfaithful and that some of the children she delivered would be the result of her prostitution. The hard request was that Hosea was to remain completely faithful to a prostitute. When she ran away, Hosea was supposed to follow after her and bring her home.

People were able to catch a glimpse of what God was doing for them when they observed the awkward pairing of an unrepentant prostitute and the prophet who fought for her. The implications of the object lesson were infinitely bigger than one man and woman. No matter what you've done, you can choose to be uncertain or you can come home.

Pray:

It can be easy to look at the unfaithfulness of others and find myself being a little judgy. Sometimes You use my discomfort to show others what Your grace and mercy look like up close and personal. Help me choose You over any other option. Help me love You more than any other person or thing. Help me refuse to choose uncertainty.

A SERIES OF VERY BAD CHOICES

Read Luke 15:11-32

Key Verse:

*"I will arise and go to my father, and will say to him,
'Father, I have sinned against heaven and before you.'"*
LUKE 15:18 NKJV

Understand:

- *Which character represents where you are at this moment? Why?*

- *Why do you think uncertain people may also be stubborn?*

Apply:

Jesus' stories helped people remember His point. Imagine two sons, one father, and some incredibly bad decisions.

One son was content to stay on the family farm and work. One father was willing to invest in the lives of his sons. He could support them. He would teach them. The second son? He liked the idea of support but didn't want to learn. He asked for an early inheritance, left home, and made a series of very bad choices. He was unfaithful with his father's gifts and came back broke, knowing he deserved nothing from his dad.

The father longed for his wayward son to return. The older brother hoped he never would. The wayward one was overwhelmingly surprised at the welcoming feast given to honor his return.

Now, change the identities of those involved in the story. The father is God. You are the wayward one. The older brother represents those who think you don't deserve a second chance.

Just remember it was the father's opinion that counted.

Pray:

It's easy to believe that the opinions of others are equal to Your opinion. While I can learn a lot from people who have a lot of life experience, they still aren't You. You tell me You love me, and You urge me to come home. Help me believe that Your offer is valid and not something You hope I decline. Make me certain that my time with You is never wasted.

THE CONVERSION OF
UNCERTAIN MOMENTS

Read Psalm 18:1–36

Key Verse:

*In my distress I called upon the LORD, and cried to my
God for help; He heard my voice out of His temple,
and my cry for help before Him came into His ears.*
PSALM 18:6 NASB

Understand:

- *What are some of the things you discovered
  in this passage that provide evidence that
  God can be trusted?*

- *How will you use something you learned
  to bring you to a place of certainty in a
  good God?*

Apply:

Uncertain times are uncertain because you don't
know how to deal with them. They present new challenges you aren't sure you want to face. They bring up
more questions than answers. And they are always
inconvenient.

Uncertain times can be found in a tax notice, a